Swept Away

by His Presence

*Refreshing the Church
with the
Power of Prayer*

Swept Away

by His Presence

*Refreshing the Church
with the
Power of Prayer*

Ron Auch

New Leaf Press

First printing: February 1998

ISBN: 0-89221-377-9
Library of Congress Catalog Number: 97-75891

Cover by Janell Robertson

This book is dedicated to

the Church of Jesus Christ,

"THE" greatest tool

for completing His work.

Contents

Part One

Chapter I

The Problem

As I sat in a crowded coffee shop across from my favorite college professor, I looked hopefully to him to clear some of the confusion that was fogging my mind. I had been an associate pastor for the past four years, but sensed God calling me to go to seminary to work on my master's degree. However, I wasn't sure where that would take me. After teaching several of the classes I had taken, Rev. Don Meyer earned my respect a dozen times over.

After Don patiently listened to my dilemma, he reached into his pocket and withdrew a pen. On an unused napkin, he drew three circles. In the first circle, he wrote an "A;" in the second, a "B;" and in the third, a "C." Looking up at me, he said, "From all that you've told me, I gather that God is indeed calling you away from your present situation. However, I can't say where God ultimately wants you."

Using his pen, he pointed down at the napkin to the circle marked "A." "Ron," he said, "This is where you are now." Moving his pen to the circle marked "B," he said, "This represents seminary." He tapped the last circle with his pen. "This represents God's ultimate will for you." As he put his pen back in his pocket, he said something that seemed quite prophetic: "God wants us at point 'C,' but the only way to get there from point 'A' is by going through point 'B.' "

That was all I needed to hear. After praying more about it, my wife and I moved from Minnesota to southeastern Wisconsin so that I could attend seminary. It was the spring of 1980, which allowed my wife and I to work all summer to raise tuition money. By the end of the summer we had not only raised enough money, but had also become deeply involved in a church.

My first day of classes coincided with the first day of a prayer seminar being taught at our church by an evangelist named Dick Eastman, whose ministry dealt solely with prayer. For some reason, there was a great expectancy in my heart which sent me rushing home from school so as not to miss any of the seminar.

That prayer seminar was the beginning of an adventure with God. I found a new, deeper love for God than I had ever had before. My newly acquired love and desire for God that I received in prayer drew me to pray even more. I even got to the point where I was skipping class to go to the prayer room, where I spent hours on end. My relationship with the Lord grew deeper than I ever thought possible as I prayed, giving myself more and more to God.

The effect prayer had on my life and ministry was equal to the effect salvation had. For several years I had been searching for ways to be more effective for God. I had placed a great deal of hope in education, but my increased knowledge left me at the same distance from God with the same effectiveness I had before. Only when I began to pray and began to truly know God did I become more effective for God.

This doesn't mean that I'm opposed to higher education. I believe that an educated man who is sensitive to the Holy Spirit can be a most powerful force for God to use. The learned Saul of Tarsus was an excellent example of this. However, we mustn't rely on higher education to do things it was never intended to do.

God was calling me to a life and ministry of prayer, and all the education in the world could not develop it.

As I think back to that meeting with Don Meyer in that coffee shop across the street from the college, I realize that God was moving me, but not to seminary. Seminary was only point "B" on my ultimate journey to point "C," a life of prayer.

The Problem

This book has been born out of a deep conviction I've held for a long time: Our pastors and churches must get back to prayer and the close relationship with God it produces or face spiritual stagnation as so many "radical" Christian movements before us have. Already we can see the first symptoms of the illness creeping through the body of the Pentecostal church: we still claim to believe in the supernatural manifestations of God's power, but we rarely see it in our services anymore.

No Vision, No Church

"Without a vision, people perish." Proverbs 29:18 teaches us that God sets each church on a path (vision). Where there is no vision, the people are unrestrained. Once they lose sight of that path, they perish. They may not cease to be; they just no longer exist with God's purposes in mind. There are many churches in every community that continue to exist in the sense that they pay their bills and have services each week, but the power has long since left.

It is with this thought that I write this book. Being an ordained minister with the Assemblies of God and having traveled this country from coast to coast teaching prayer seminars for several years, I can see that we are in dire need of prayer. If a person were to compare how often our ministers preached on the subject of the baptism of the Holy Spirit in days gone by, to how often they preach about it today, it would not be difficult to see a trend. Some have said that within one decade there will no longer be any preaching on the baptism of the Holy Spirit in our churches.

It is my prayer that we never lose sight of why God raised

us up. If we lose our vision, we perish. Interestingly enough, one of the Hebrew meanings for the word "perish" is "go back." Without a vision the people of God "go back" to what they used to be. Then God will raise up another people to take the Pentecostal message to the ends of the earth.

In this, the first part of the book, we will examine the problem, which as you will see we must diagnose as the prayerlessness of today's church. We are in an age when we desperately need churches that know how to storm heaven, and pastors who know their God. We need prayer.

Chapter II

The Power Encounter

Without experience, nothing can be known suffi-ciently. — Roger Bacon, 16th century philosopher

Meanwhile, Saul was still breathing out murderous threats against the Lord's disciples. He went to the high priest and asked him for letters to the synagogues in Damascus, so that if he found any there who belonged to the Way, whether men or women, he might take them as prisoners to Jerusalem. As he neared Damascus on his journey, suddenly a light from heaven flashed around him. He fell to the ground and heard a voice say to him, "Saul, Saul, why do you persecute me?" "Who are you, Lord?" Saul asked. "I am Jesus, whom you are persecuting," he replied. "Now get up and go into the city and you will be told what you must do" (Acts 9:1-6).

Saul was one of those people who was anything but average. You know the type. Even as a youth, he had things a little better than the other Jewish kids. He wasn't schooled in synagogue with the other children by some generic rabbi. Instead, he attached himself as a pupil to Gamaliel, one of the most famous and revered rabbis in Israel. It was like being taught physics by Albert Einstein. Any boy in Saul's position was headed in only one direction: *up!* From childhood on Saul seemed destined to have his name etched in the "Who's Who in Jewish Synagogues" scrolls.

But Saul's climb up the ladder of success was abruptly halted when he ran head-on with the resurrected Messiah whose followers he was persecuting in a bloodthirsty exhibition of Jewish zealotry. Something happened on that road to Damascus that caused this young up-and-coming Pharisee to forsake all the popularity and respect he had struggled so hard to gain.

Saul experienced what is called a "power encounter" with Christ. When he met Christ, it turned his world upside-down. The course of his life turned 180 degrees. By this, I don't mean that he only experienced God's redemptive grace.

Though that is true, more than that took place. He experienced a thorough transformation which reversed his concept of right and wrong. His hopes, his hates, his dreams, and his desires all radically changed. This was proven when he turned his back on all that he had spent his life attaining, in order to — of all things — wander the length and breadth of the Roman Empire preaching about salvation through the same Jesus he formerly persecuted so ruthlessly.

Saul's contemporaries could not understand why a man of Saul's caliber and potential would abandon such a promising future in order to fanatically preach what he had just fanatically persecuted. It was something none of them could even begin to fathom. It is also, unfortunately, an experience which many Pentecostals are losing sight of today.

In the Beginning

At its outset, however, the power encounter hallmarked the Pentecostal church. This movement's greatest distinction in its first generation was its adherents' powerful encounters with God. The book *Anointed to Serve* by Dr. William W. Menzies illustrates this point as it documents the birth of the Pentecostal movement, at 312 Azusa Street, Los Angeles in 1906.

Odd as it may seem, according to eyewitness accounts published in this book, those early Pentecostal meetings were completely unorthodox and, by some of today's standards, utterly doomed for failure.

The Azusa Street Revival, as it is sometimes called, did not take place in the most beautiful church in town. Quite the contrary. It was held in an old, unattractive, two-story frame building which had been used most recently as a livery stable and tenement house, compared inside and out to a barn by some. Inside this humble shack there was no gorgeously garbed choir, nor was there a finely tuned orchestra. What's more, no hand bills were distributed, nor was there any other kind of public advertising employed to promote the revival meetings.

However, God was there, manifesting himself without any kind of restrictions. That was enough to draw people. Altar calls were announced simply and matter-of-factly, without coaxing, cajoling, or psychological wheedling. Holy Spirit-wrought conviction drove the lost to the altars where they found their God. Those who came to Christ embarked on their new spiritual journey with incredible zeal and phenomenal enthusiasm. Nothing else seemed to matter. A love for the pleasures of this world was dwarfed and swallowed up by this new exciting life with their risen Saviour.

Some of those gathered heard the voices of angels singing praises to the Most High, while others in attendance sang praises composed by the Holy Spirit. Physical laws were bent like silly putty as the sick were instantly healed of their afflictions. Meanwhile, others were engulfed in the resplendent presence of God, praising God in languages foreign to their own ears. Many fell prostrate and worshiped God with other languages given to them by the Holy Spirit.

No one ever knew what was going to happen next, claimed

on-the-spot reports in *Anointed to Serve*. There was no liturgy, no pattern — just order; God's order, not man's. Those individuals who moved out of that divine order were quickly righted with but a word from Rev. W.J. Seymore, the leader of the meeting, who delivered the preaching.

Portrait of a Skeptic

At Azusa Street, when people accepted Jesus as their personal Saviour and made Him Lord of their lives, it was exciting, to say the least. It was never so mundane as to be forgotten about quickly. Dr. Menzies chronicles one such encounter in his book involving a newspaper reporter assigned to cover the revival meeting, which he and his editors regarded as a gathering of psychotic religious fanatics. The reporter in question was as completely amused as his editors by the idea of writing an exploitative article dripping with sensationalism. (It was business-as-usual for the "yellow journalists" of the era's notorious "penny press.") But after the man arrived on the scene, the situation took a dramatic turn.

The Holy Spirit moved this journalist deeply as he observed the stirring scenes which were the norm at Azusa Street. Suddenly, an elderly woman shouted something in a language alien to everyone — except this foreign-born reporter, that is. He heard and understood her as she described his sinful past in his native tongue, without accent or error. Very shortly, he realized that what had taken place was supernatural and that it happened in order to draw him to God. During that service, he repented of his sin and accepted Jesus Christ as his personal Saviour and Lord.

Going straight from the meeting, he informed his employers that he could not write the sensational article they wanted, but offered to write an impartial account. As you might expect, his employers were not thrilled by his offer. In fact, they petulantly informed him that they had no need for such an article or the writer of it. Although he lost his job that night, he found his eternal destiny and went home that night the happiest unemployed journalist in the world.

Lest You Forget

These powerful experiences, which set the Pentecostals apart and made them the most radical element in Christianity, served as a reference point for each Pentecostal. During times of tribulation, each individual was able to look back at that day when he met Christ and was encouraged instantly as he was reminded of his purpose as a Christian. He began his life as a Christian by powerfully meeting God, as that reporter at Azusa Street did. Very little else mattered to him aside from Jesus. He met a powerful God who revolutionized his life, as was the case with Paul. Such a newly born Christian saw no reason for this to change. For the rest of his life, his purpose was to know his God in His power and to fellowship with Him.

The movement also had a collective purpose: to introduce the world to God as He is: real, conscious, and, to a certain degree, quite tangible. They ran into conflict with the notion that God should be worshiped and recognized on man's terms, as a God who was "somewhere up there," but who ("perhaps fortunately") didn't intervene in the lives of men.

One considering this period in history must realize that during this era it appeared to many that the old relic called "religion" was on its way out, while science was on its way in. Charles Darwin's theory of evolution was catching on big in Europe and was just establishing a foothold in the scientific community in the United States. Many finally made the transition from passive Christianity to atheism and agnosticism because finally, it was supposed, science had proved that the Bible was a long-lived collection of myths. Man finally had a "rational" reason to do away with God.

At this time, most of the mainline denominations offered services that could be certified and approved by such "enlightened" skeptics. By this I mean that atheists could have attended these services without batting an eyelash (today we call them "seeker-friendly" services). With one eyebrow smugly arched, they could have explained away those "primitive rituals" (and did!). They did this with such ease and assurance because they observed nothing happening in a Christian "ritual" that they could not observe in a Hindu or lslamic "ritual." People sang. People made speeches (which the Christians called "sermons").

In the case of any of these "rituals," all was centered on a God who showed no signs of existing. As far as many learned scholars were concerned, one Christian church was pretty much like any other religious group. It was just a gathering of people doing things any atheist could have done: singing, speaking, and so forth. Such man-oriented, man-limited services were the norm — until the Pentecostal movement surfaced.

The Pentecostals dared to invite their God to become a very active participant in their services instead of just a dubious mute observer sitting in some kind of spiritual grandstand. Such divine involvement yielded frustration for skeptics who were left grasping at straws to explain such goings-on. Some abandoned their skepticism to meet their eternal destiny, while only the most stubborn continued to grasp at their scientific straws.

The first years of the 20th century were glorious days for those called "Pentecostals." The flame and fire of the Holy Spirit blazed through their ranks and on into the hurting world. They introduced the world to a real God, laying waste to numerous religious ceremonies and the impersonal worship being carried out in the name of Christ. Yet, these first generation Christians fell short of fulfilling one crucial obligation.

> Only be careful and watch yourselves closely so
> that you do not forget the things your eyes have seen or
> let them slip from your heart as long as you live. Teach
> them to your children and to their children after them
> (Deut. 4:9).

Although they continued to live and breathe for the purposes of knowing God and making Him known, not forgetting the things they had seen, they did not truly make them known to their children and to their children after them. A breakdown in communication occurred in this area because they failed to teach their children the importance of prayer. Prayer was the catalyst that caused the remarkable manifestations of the Holy Spirit at Azusa Street. It was prayer that fanned into flame all those power encounters subsequent to salvation. Without prayer, none of these Pentecostal distinctions would have ever bloomed.

It is very important for us to realize why those first generation Christians prayed if we are ever to understand why most Christians today do not pray. Those first generation Christians had a ravenous hunger to spiritually experience their God. That's how they first met Jesus, and they never wanted to lose sight of that. Furthermore, they knew that a power encounter with God was subsequent to prayer, so they prayed.

Their children, however, were at a disadvantage in the area of prayer. They didn't have the motivation to pray that their parents did. Unlike their parents, these second generation Christians did not have a power encounter at salvation. They grew up in a Christian home, living under biblical standards of morality. Then, at some point, they surrendered their lives to Christ and were saved. However, they did not experience the Lord's power. They did experience His redemptive grace through the shed blood of Jesus Christ, but not His power. The first generation experienced it because great power was needed to change their lives. Their children and grandchildren, however, were already living by biblical morals and so were not required to change to the same extent. Therefore, they didn't experience God's power as their predecessors did.

The second generation Christians who accepted Christ were saved, but that's about all. They didn't hunger after an experience with God (which can be seen only in prayer). How could they? Have you ever had a craving for sautéed snails? Probably not. You can't hunger after something you've never tasted. Therefore, they had neither the motivation to pray, nor an understanding of how important prayer is.

Because so many in the second generation prayed infrequently, they did not have the awesome power and person of the

Holy Spirit manifested as their parents did. They didn't witness remarkable signs and wonders with the frequency or intensity that their parents did. The extent to which the power of the Holy Spirit was manifested was proportional to the extent that they prayed.

In My Life

I am a first generation Christian. I wasn't born in a church, nor was I quoting Scripture at that time. When I met Jesus Christ in January of 1973, I hadn't attended church regularly for over ten years. When I met Christ on that cold, snowy day in January, my life turned 180 degrees. Like young Saul, I had a power encounter with Christ. That experience is my reference point. I can look back at (or "refer to") that time and instantly be reminded of my purpose as a Christian: to know God powerfully. As long as I keep that experience fresh in my mind and renew it in my heart daily through prayer, l will always find purpose in being a Christian.

However, my son, a second generation Christian, is growing up in an environment that is entirely different from the one his dad grew up in. He is often in church with me four times in one week. If he becomes part of the usual cycle, he will grow up with a biblically based philosophy of life. He'll do his best to observe all the "do's" and "don'ts" of the Bible. His salvation experience will not be the same as mine. His life won't change like mine did. He'll just get saved and continue with life as usual. His reference point will not be a powerful meeting with God; it will be the Christian lifestyle he's grown up with.

However, he doesn't have to be swept away by this cycle. This cycle is a tendency, not an inevitability. I can help prevent him from falling into the cycle by teaching him the things I have seen. In fact, it is my responsibility to do so, even as it was the responsibility of the ancient Israelites to pass down to their descendants the things they had seen. My son needs to know that his dad was an evil man who was saved by God's grace. He needs to know that if it were not for Jesus Christ's coming into my life, he could possibly be growing up in a non-Christian home. I must tell him about my power encounter with Christ and make sure that he understands we have a powerful God who intervenes in the affairs of men.

If I do this, my reference point can influence his life greatly. He will be able to look back to my power encounter and see his purpose as a Christian. The apostle Paul was constantly doing this. He used his own testimony to stir the church and the world. When a person has a proper reference point, they tend to pray more and, subsequently, meet God more powerfully. A person certainly doesn't have to be unsaved to meet God powerfully. God is met in prayer.

If I don't influence my son with my own reference point, his reference point will differ so greatly from mine that we will have two entirely different approaches to the work of God. He could very well be involved in the work of God, but his perspective of what is important in the ministry will be so different from mine that our ministries would be completely antithetical to each other.

I am seeing this ministry contrast in our Pentecostal churches. We now have many second generation preachers and even some third. Their approach to the ministry today is vastly different from the approach to the ministry our founders had.

Truth and Consequences

As a consequence of this cycle, the objectives of the church in general began to change. How could Pentecostal churches carry out a mission founded on power encounters when they were not being experienced nearly as much? Of course, they could not, and since most had never tasted prayer-wrought Pentecost, most had no appetite for it. Their reference point was vastly different from their parents'. They couldn't look back at a life-changing time of salvation and see their purpose in life as their parents did. However, they could look back at the godly lifestyle they lived all their lives. Thus, lifestyle became their reference point. Subsequently, they became fine citizens and upstanding members of their church, but they lacked the same kind of zeal their parents had.

I have taught the need of the first generation to pass down its reference point to the second generation on many occasions. One of these particularly sticks out in my mind. A woman once approached me after the service to talk to me about her family. She said that her entire family came to know Christ through the dramatic healing of her mother-in-law. It was a powerful experience that deeply touched that entire generation of her family. Then with a slight tremor in her voice, she said, "I never told my boys about this. All I offered them was the Christian lifestyle. I believe that's why both of them have chosen another lifestyle."

This does not mean that the second generation had faith in a gospel of works any more than the first generation believed they were saved by their powerful encounters with Christ. In both generations, salvation by grace through the shed blood of Jesus Christ was taught and believed. The trouble starts after salvation when one asks, "What is life all about now that I'm saved?" Since the second generation rarely experiences God's power and doesn't understand the importance of prayer, they cannot assume that what follows salvation should be a life centered on communing with God deeply and powerfully. They are left with a focus on living life in a way that lines up with biblical standards.

The third generation has met with the same fate of prayerlessness that their parents did, and because of this, today we have a relatively powerless Pentecost. Most Pentecostals believe in the supernatural, but seldom see it. Most pastors are unable to pray successfully for people to be delivered from their bondage or for the sick to be healed.

I have no ax to grind with second or third generation Christians. They can't help being born when they were and not receiving instruction on prayer. The problem we're dealing with is really a first generation problem. The second and third generations are just innocent victims of a first generation error.

Hope

There is hope for second and third generation Christians. With God, there is always hope. If it were not so, I would greatly fear for my son, who is a second generation Christian in a third generation movement. However, he's not doomed to be a wishy-washy second generation type Christian just because he won't meet Christ as powerfully as I did. He has the potential to be a Christian walking very closely with God. How? I must teach him that he can have a power encounter subsequent to salvation through prayer. My son will never meet Christ the same way I did, but he can experience God just as powerfully through prayer.

As I said earlier, second and third generation Christians are at a disadvantage because they don't have the same motivation to pray as their forefathers. But that doesn't mean they can't or won't pray. All it means is that they need the instruction of a first generation believer. This means that my son, for example, needs me to provide the motivation and instruction to get him started in a life centered on communicating with his Heavenly Father. What remains for him is to pray and develop a prayer life that will become his reference point or power encounter.

I have mentioned that second and third generations have an improper reference point. This is generally true, but there are a few exceptions. You and the Lord are the only ones who really know what your reference point is. If you are a second or third generation Christian (or even a first) who lacks power in his walk with God, prayer is the solution. Only in that divine communication can the believer really encounter his Creator in His glory. It is the key to the power encounter. Without it, we will change directions as a movement.

Chapter III

Cisterns That Hold No Water

I am rich; I have acquired wealth and do not need a thing. — Church of Laodicia, A.D. 96

It was an era in which people only dreamed of television, and only the most imaginative did that; an era that neither witnessed nor heard of world wars, to say nothing of nuclear weapons capable of devastating the surface of the entire planet. It was a world during which old-timers waited for that "horseless buggy fad" to come to the halt they predicted. Yet, it was in the "primitive" society of the early 1900s that an evangelist named Gladys Pearson preached a startling warning, a warning which spelled out an eventual decline and decay for the movement called "Pentecostal."

It is a warning that has gone unheeded through the decades and one which, if unheeded, will serve as an epitaph for this movement in the near future. It is this fearsome warning that will serve as a basis for this chapter in an effort to clearly explain why our movement is in such grave trouble.

27

The Patriarchal Parallel

When Abram was ninety-nine years old, the Lord appeared to him and said, "I am God Almighty; walk before me and be blameless. I will confirm my covenant between me and you and will greatly increase your numbers." Abram fell face down, and God said to him, "As for me, this is my covenant with you. You will be the father of many nations. No longer will you be called Abram; your name will be 'Abraham,' for I have made you a father of many nations" (Gen. 17:1-5).

It was during the generation of Abraham that God began to do something new. Abraham was in the first generation of this new covenant relationship with God. Abraham could be likened to those early believers who met at Azusa Street. They, too, were the first generation to experience something new that God was doing. Their parents had never seen the likes of it, nor had their grandparents. They were pioneers, embarking on a spiritual voyage with no recent earthly precedent, just as Abraham was.

By studying Abraham, we can see certain characteristics that are shared universally by first generation believers. They are characteristics common to all such believers regardless of comparative cultural or technological variations. The chief thing we notice about Abraham is that he was an altar builder. He almost couldn't make it through a single chapter of Genesis without building an altar. This shouldn't be viewed as some sort of architectural zeal which consumed Abraham. It has much more spiritual significance than that.

Altar building is symbolic of prayer, or perhaps we could say that prayer is symbolic of building. In either case, there is a direct relationship. Abraham built numerous altars so that he could worship God and sacrifice to Him. Wasn't he building altars to accomplish the same ends we are when we pray? Of course he was. Although we do not need sacrifices to atone for our sins (we already have One), we offer the sacrifice of self when we pray.

Abraham possessed the spirit of a prayer warrior, manifesting that spirit everywhere he went as he built altar after altar to sacrifice to God. This urgency and zeal after prayer is business as usual for first generation believers like Abraham. These believers are establishing a new movement and are constantly on the offensive, blazing trails for their descendants.

Abraham had one other very noticeable penchant: digging wells. If Abraham went through an entire chapter of Genesis without building an altar, then he dug a well instead. As was the case earlier, Abraham's actions did not reflect a love for construction work. His wells were a reflection of his desire to bless others. Any one of those wells would have indeed been a blessing for someone on one of those sweltering days the Middle East is known for. Those wells also symbolized a great deal of hard work and self-denial.

Unfortunately, both of these traits began to fade in the subsequent generations. His descendants didn't exactly follow in his footsteps, but instead luxuriated in the land God gave to their father, who was a millionaire in his day because of God's kindness to him.

For the first generation of any movement, the prayer and self-sacrifice Abraham practiced with such fervor are musts. They pray. And pray. And pray and pray. They have no blessings initially. The only thing they can offer God at the altar is themselves. But as time marches on, and as God is faithful, blessings come to them as surely as they came for Abraham. Then, like Abraham, they begin to dig wells. Blessings come for their children as their churches become more organized and better-equipped. But the second generation simply walks in on the blessings, and that's when the trouble starts.

The Spiritual Generation Gap

In the patriarchal case we've been studying, Isaac was the second generation. Because his father, Abraham, was a man who diligently sought after God, Isaac was the recipient of fabulous blessings. Psalms 112 teaches us that the children of those that greatly fear God will be mighty on earth. Abraham, Isaac's father, was a well-digger of the first order. Abraham feared his God which resulted in a life of consecration. He had also invested his life establishing something for Isaac to move into, freeing him from the weighty burden of starting from scratch.

However, this freedom is not entirely beneficial. It carries with it some drawbacks. For instance, the second generation doesn't place the same priority on "altar-building" and "well-digging" that the first generation does. The ideas of sacrifice and self-denial are not a must for them. Similarly, prayer is not held in the high esteem that it was a generation before. This is due, at least in part, to the comfortable setting they've stepped into. There's no struggling to build a church in their case. Everything is pretty much downhill. At least for them it is, but their children will not receive any blessings because you cannot establish blessings for the next generation without prayer. If you try, the "wells" you dig will hold no water.

It is without prayer that the second generation tries to improve upon what the first generation accomplished. When prayerless Isaac did this, he ran into trouble:

> Isaac's servants dug in the valley and discovered a well of fresh water there. But the herdsmen of Gerar quarreled with Isaac's herdsmen and said, "The water is ours." So he named the well Esek [dispute, strife], because they disputed with him. Then they dug another well, but they quarreled over that one also; so he named it Sitnah [opposition, envy] (Gen. 26:19-20).

This is a textbook case of man without prayer trying to improve upon a plan God established in a people of prayer. Isaac, not a prayer warrior like his father, tried to improve upon his dad's work and collided with envy and strife (human problems).

Yet, there is more to this story. In the previous verse we are informed that "Isaac reopened wells that had been dug in the time of his father Abraham" (Gen. 26:18). That was where Isaac found the blessings. Later, when he dug new wells he received only envy and strife. It was then that Isaac did something different, something most second generationists don't do: he realized that his father's way (the way of prayer) was the only way. He went back to his father's wells. Unfortunately, most second generation believers don't do this. Most forge on ahead, trying to improve upon that which was founded on prayer, *without* prayer.

This is not really a case of conspiratory rebellion. These subsequent believers are not fighting against what their parents began. It's just that their spiritual circumstances are nothing like their parents' were. It's difficult for these young people who have received so many blessings to grasp what their parents went through. They were never victims of egg-hurling scorners, as their parents were. They can't relate to that. Neither can they relate to having nothing but God. No, because of the blessings they have received, they do not face the same circumstances which helped to shape their parents' faith. It's because they don't really understand what their elders held most important that they try to "improve" upon things.

I recall speaking to a pastor (a second generation Pentecostal) once who confirmed this suspicion of mine. When he grew up, family camp was the place to go. Anybody who was anybody in the church went to family camp. However, family camp was an experience he came to dread because of his ultra-strict father who forbade him from even moving his eyes from the platform. If his father caught him so much as glancing at one of the other children in the building, it meant a spanking. As a result of this, when he became a father, he never steered his children toward family camp for fear that the slightest coaxing might recreate his own childhood problem for his children.

Of course, I'd have to say that this pastor's father was quite extremist in his disciplinary measures, but this story is not meant to be taken as a lesson in child-rearing. The point of the story is that the older man was adamant in the extreme about something, and his son was never able to understand why. This is very typical in first/second generation relations. The first generation becomes quite ardent about certain things because they paid a great price for their faith.

The problem with this elder group is that they assume that their descendants will automatically understand why they feel as strongly as they do about certain issues, but their children will never just automatically know. They can't. Their world and the spiritual environment in which they grow up is so different that they can't just somehow end up walking the same path. Sadly enough, though, because the first generation assumes they understand, they never take the time to explain it to their children, and from here, the problem snowballs.

The Schemers

The result is a movement which has changed in all but name from what it was at its inception. It may still hold to its original doctrine, but the fire is gone. By this time what was a must for the first generation and a convenience for the second becomes nonsense to the third.

All this talk about doing things the old way makes no sense to the average third generation believer. The old ways, it is said, are for the old days, and the new days require new ways. The third generation believers claim that in this area we are dealing with cultural issues, when we are not. Prayer is not a cultural issue. It transcends all cultures, societies, and ages. It should be basic to every generation everywhere.

In addition, the third generation becomes a group of schemers, like Jacob, their equivalent in Genesis. They scheme to cover a lack of holiness under the guise of cultural differences, personal tastes, individual backgrounds, and individual pasts. Like Jacob, they become deceivers and supplanters. They are always scouting out new ways, while ignoring the old way, the way of prayer.

Anyone who went to Sunday school as a child knows the story of how Jacob conned his brother Esau into giving him his birthright. Eventually Jacob was brought face to face again with the brother he slickered so many years earlier. The last thing Jacob heard his brother say was something about how he was going to kill him. It was something everyone — including Jacob — took seriously, for it was then that his mother sent him away to marry one of Laban's daughters. In Genesis 32, Jacob was about to come face to face not just with his brother, but also with his own deceit.

At this point Jacob was fearing for his life. He doubted that his chicanery had slipped Esau's mind over the years. (It's funny how things like that stick in people's minds, isn't it?) He had to do something. As was natural for him, he did things his way instead of God's way. He tried to buy his brother off, or to put it more delicately in his own words, "I will pacify him with special gifts." This is par for the course for the third generation believer. For him, the password is "MONEY." It is looked upon as the cure-all. (Of course, to keep things spiritual he must reaffirm that it is God who supplies his monetary "fix." Greed and materialism are then elevated to the status of theology.)

> So, Jacob's gifts went on ahead of him, but he himself spent the night in the camp. That night Jacob got up and took his two wives, his two maidservants and his eleven sons and crossed the ford of the Jabbok. After he had sent them across the stream, he sent over all his possessions. So Jacob was left alone, and a man wrestled with him till daybreak. (Gen. 32:21-23)

The phrase "Jacob was left alone" is significant. There was nobody else around, no one to talk to, and nothing in particular to do. It's at these moments in our lives that we are left with no choice but to confront ourselves with who we really are. For Jacob, as for many of us, it was no easy task. The Book of Genesis tells us that an angel wrestled with Jacob all night. I'm sure that Jacob was not just wrestling with an angel that night. He was also wrestling with himself. He looked deep inside himself and didn't like what he saw. He wanted to change.

Consequently, he would not let go of the angel for fear that he would come out of the ordeal the same old Jacob. He politely informed the angel of this, to which the angel finally responded, "What is your name?" At this point, Jacob had to humble his pride and admit, "I am Jacob." It was humbling because his name was synonymous with "supplanter," or more colloquially, "con-niver." At that moment he was changed, and to bear witness to this the angel declared, "You will no longer be the supplanter; you will now be Israel."

What changed Jacob was admitting who and what he was. It was a moment of admittance and repentance, and it was his own decision to return to the wells of his grandfather Abraham. After this, he knew true blessings from above, from the Father of heavenly lights, from the Lord of love. These blessings were al-ready established, but he could not receive them until he admit-ted the error of his ways and returned to the old, true ways.

The results of Jacob's transformation were really quite amaz-ing. To begin with, he no longer feared his brother because when our relationship with God is right, we do not fear men. Besides that, his brother forgave him and ceased carrying a grudge. It was a fulfillment of a proverb a man named "Solomon" would write centuries later: "When a man's way please the Lord, He makes even his enemies to be at peace with him" (Prov. 16:7).

The story concludes by telling how Esau ran to meet Jacob and embraced him, throwing his arms around his neck and kiss-ing him as they wept together. What a reunion. Unfortunately, it is a very isolated case because so few will humble themselves as Jacob did to return to the old way of prayer.

Broken Cisterns

The prophet Jeremiah quoted the Lord as saying, "My people have committed two sins: they have forsaken me, the spring of living water, and have dug their own cisterns, broken cisterns that cannot hold water" (Jer. 2:13). This same problem arises time after time throughout the history of God's dealings with man. It has happened from the time of the patriarchs to this very day. God's people wander away from Him and His ways and hatch their own plans and strategies based on man's limited perception of reality. They do things their way, not caring to so much as utter a word to God (that's called "prayer") about it to seek His advice.

Jeremiah clarified the problem by saying, "Does a maiden forget her jewelry, a bride her wedding ornaments? Yet my people have forgotten me, days without number" (Jer. 2:32). These comparisons were being used to make God's people see how absurd it was for them to cease seeking after God in all their doings. For one of God's people to quit seeking Him whole-heartedly would be like a bride marching down the aisle to "Here Comes the Bride" without her wedding gown. It would be like a woman of meager means nonchalantly casting her pieces of fine jewelry down a wishing well.

Such scenarios simply aren't natural. They're strange and bizarre — almost as much as the people of God not praying and pursuing God with all their heart. Such a people cut themselves off from the Spring of Living Water and subsequently have nothing with which to fill their cisterns. What is left is an empty shell, merely an empty hull of theology.

In many areas of the Pentecostal movement, that's all that is left. See for yourself how often we talk about peace and yet are afraid of the future. We talk about the strength of the Lord yet more Christian marriages are breaking up than ever before. If we do not purpose in our hearts to seek God with all of our being, this will become our status quo. We will have nothing to offer people besides empty theology, little more than a weak religious philosophy. The power of God will have seeped through the prayer walls of the cistern.

Any people guilty of this first sin will also be guilty of the second one Jeremiah mentioned: digging their own cisterns — broken cisterns that cannot hold water. This is to say that since they have quit seeking God, the Spring of Living Water, they're going to have to get their "water" someplace else. They'll be forced to dig their own cisterns. But God warns that cisterns dug by men cannot hold water. Yet, many in our movement are frantically digging their own cisterns.

By and large, our movement has rejected praying and seeking God as a viable, realistic, practical solution to the problems of life. Instead of seeking God, we're contriving our own inferior game plan. Since we don't really believe God will faithfully respond to our prayer, we no longer visit the sick to see God heal them, even though that was God's game plan in the New Testament. Instead, we visit the sick to encourage them and boost their morale. There's nothing wrong with encouraging people and so on, but only if it is not to the exclusion of God's plan. It is because of our empty wells that we have no more power to minister to people than the ungodly.

Christians did not always run around looking diligently for ways to minister to people without prayer. It was exactly the opposite in the early days of our movement. At that time, saints realized that God has complete, total, and unlimited power. This being the case, it was only logical to seek the solution to any given problem in God. That's why their ministry was so successful.

For example, John Hyde (Praying Hyde), a former missionary to India, habitually invested his best time in prayer. It was in prayer that he sensed God placing a challenge before him to win one soul every day. One year later, he had personally led over 400 people to Jesus. He then felt prompted to win two people to Christ each day. By the end of his life, he was leading four people to Christ every day.

It's Hyde's philosophy that has interested me greatly. His approach to soul-winning was based on emulating Christ. When he was no longer effective on the streets he went back to the prayer closet. Hyde believed that his ineffectiveness was because he no longer reflected Christ. He believed he should get so close to Christ through prayer that Jesus in him would attract people to himself. Today, if we are not as effective as we would like to be, we go back to the drawing board and devise a different way to evangelize. We don't go back to the prayer closet so we can look more like our Saviour. We have come to believe we are ineffective because we look too much like Him already. The church is trying to distance itself from the image of Christ.

Isn't it fascinating to think that John Hyde, a man of prayer, felt that the most effective way to draw people to Christ was to look like Christ, while today's relatively prayerless church has come to believe that the most effective way to draw people away from the world is through looking like the world. We have entire "Christian" industries which justify their worldly look and sound to this very philosophy. This is indeed strange, especially coming from an organization that has its roots in a holiness movement.

The unhappy result is that Christians cannot be distinguished from non-Christians. Moreover, the world sees little hope for them in us. Those who come to Christ do so because Christ offers them something different from what they already have. I learned this lesson the hard way during a hospital call made on behalf of my church. At the hospital I spoke to a teenage girl who had attempted suicide. Upon entering her hospital room I noticed that every square inch of wall space was obscured by secular rock music posters. Our church was about to sponsor a "Christian rock concert," so I decided to invite the girl. Just as I was about to invite her, the Holy Spirit spoke to my heart saying, "You want to offer her an imitation of the world and its trappings that led her to attempt suicide?" I began to realize that what this girl needed was something completely different from what she already had. She needed Jesus, not some worldly version of Christianity.

The world is looking for something different from what it already has, but if we do not again become a people who zealously go after God, we will never have that "something different" to offer them. Psychologists will be able to offer them as much as we do and we will be left alone and confused with a stale religion which offers neither the power to change men's lives nor the strength to maintain our own lagging momentum. We will dig empty wells which produce empty relationships with Christ.

The Key Generation

What I have described thus far is a cycle. It is a pattern of events which repeats itself at regular intervals. Importantly, it is a cycle which only lasts three generations, meaning that at the end of the third generation it can be expected to start all over again with a new move by God. This makes the first and third generations the key generations. I believe this is why Abraham (first generation) and Jacob (third generation) had their names changed, while Isaac (second generation) did not.

If we examine Abram carefully, we will see that he needed a drastic change in his life. God needed to do some work on him before this man would be able to be the earthly head of a brand new plan of God. He needed to be a man of power and strength. He needed a power encounter with God to bring this about, and he had it. Then, symbolic as a new beginning and a new destiny as "the father of many nations," God changed his name to "Abraham."

Isaac, on the other hand, had no real need to change. He grew up in the midst of a revival of sorts. He had all the blessings. He had it made in the shade. All he had to do was sustain the revival through prayer, but he failed to do this. It is because Isaac failed to sustain the revival through prayer that his descendant, Jacob, was in need of a power encounter. Therefore, the third generation becomes most crucial because these people will usher in the next generation, the generation which will begin the cycle all over again with a revival.

That brings us to one last issue for us to consider: Joseph (a type of Christ), the fourth generation, the generation of revival. Typically, fourth generation Christians have gotten so far away from the faith of their great grandfathers that their experience with the Lord is unrelated to them. They have a brand new perspective which is very much like a first generation Christian. The cycle begins anew.

Fourth generation Christians have nothing but God. They seem to have a new hunger, a new drive and desire. They want God, so they pray. Without a new excitement for prayer no move of God can continue with the same fire it began with. Let's be the generation that turns things around.

Chapter IV

Sophistication:
The Holy Spirit
of Today's Church

The church that is man-managed instead of God-governed is doomed to failure. A ministry that is college-trained, but not Spirit-filled works no miracles.
— Samuel Chadwick, revivalist

When I was in college I had a history professor who introduced his ancient history course with the immortal words, "If there is one thing we learn from history, it is that we do not learn from history. We repeat the same mistakes over and over." The more I consider that statement, the more I see its truth. Sadly, it is particularly true in the Church of Jesus Christ.

Every four generations, a radical Christian movement surfaces, particularized by the zeal of its constituency and its adherence to supernatural experiences with God, while the existing denominations avert or roll their theological eyes. Then, because the subsequent generations do not pray, that same movement degenerates and, by its third generation, has lost all the phenomenal distinctions that made it so radical. A study of church history and the Scriptures clearly demonstrates this pattern and proves that up to this point in time, every fiery Christian movement has lost its fire by its third generation.

Jonathan Wesley was aware of this cycle. In fact, he feared that his movement, which was in the midst of a blazing revival, would follow the unfortunate way of every other prior movement. In 1786 he wrote, "I am not afraid that people called Methodists should ever cease to exist either in Europe or America. But I am afraid, lest they should only exist as a dead sect, having the form of religion without the power." Certainly we Pentecostals should be as humble as Wesley.

If every other movement has become diluted by its third generation, why won't the same happen to us? I hope and pray that we are not so arrogant as to consider ourselves completely immune to the forces which have injured those movements that came before us. At present, the Pentecostal church for the most part is in its third generation and is on the same road to conservatism its many predecessors traveled on their way to spiritual stagnation.

Wanted: Replacement for the Holy Spirit

As we've seen, our Pentecostal churches are moving further and further away from experience and moving closer and closer to carefully planned, predictable services based almost entirely on human talent and efforts. Many churches have seemingly limited the gifts of the Holy Spirit to speaking in tongues. In some churches, even that is forbidden. The sad fact is that the power of the Holy Spirit is seldom, if ever seen — dramatically or otherwise in our churches — all stemming from the lack of prayer.

Because the Holy Spirit is not functioning in these churches as He should, they are searching for a replacement for Him, something that can draw people to the church. Enter sophistication, the Holy Spirit of today's church.

Today, we broadcast Christianity on every conceivable medium, hoping that it will do the work of the Holy Spirit. We feel confident that our mass mechanization can draw people to the Lord. Forty percent ($200 million) of all the money raised for the gospel each year goes to Christian television and yet only 3 percent of those in our churches were won to the Lord through it. Any business man can tell you that is not a good return on your money. In fact, it is wasting it.

Prayer and the Holy Spirit are still acknowledged as important and even necessary in our churches, but neither are often seen. If they were truly depended upon, modern Christians would spend infinitely more time on their knees.

For Sale (Cheap!): The Fruit of the Spirit

This heretical replacement is evident in many preachers today. At one time, the fruit of the Holy Spirit established the credibility of a preacher. If someone was visiting a church for the first time, he would determine the pastor's legitimacy by asking questions like, "Does this man have love? Does he have joy? Self control?" If he didn't, he was no man of God because the absence of the fruit of the Spirit in his life was a sure indicator that he was spending a woefully inadequate amount of time in prayer. And who would want pastor who didn't spend great amounts of time in prayer? If, on the other hand, a man exemplified the fruit of the Spirit, people accepted his ministry because it was obvious that he was a praying pastor, and that's the kind of pastor a believer wanted.

Today, however, many Pentecostals ignore these things. We have become accustomed to the "saintly celebrities" our sophistication has produced for our secular media. Most believers are looking for a preacher with a sparkling personality and oratory gifts similar to TV personalities in the secular media. We have mistakenly substituted personalities and polished showmanship for the anointing.

By today's standards, anyone can buy the anointing. It's called "air time." Any pastor, evangelist, or preacher who can afford to pay the monetary price can become an anointed man of

God (or so we think). Consequently, anything anybody says on Christian television is considered straight from God.

However, the anointing was not such a marketable commodity in the New Testament:

> When Simon saw that the Spirit was given at the laying on of the apostles' hands, he offered them money and said, "Give me also this ability so that everyone on whom I lay my hands may receive the Holy Spirit." Peter answered: "May your money perish with you, because you thought you could buy the gift of God with money! You have no part or share in this ministry, because your heart is not right before God (Acts 8:18-21).

The Pentecostal movement began with a powerful wave of the Holy Spirit. Because of this, it also began with powerful men of God who would have responded to Simon much as Peter did. Today, unfortunately, we are left with many preachers who are much more like Simon than they are like the Apostle. It is very desirable today to have the masses think that the touch of God is on your life and ministry. But it is not desirable to invest time in God's presence to receive that divine touch. It is not only more fashionable but also easier to depend upon creativity, showmanship, and personality instead of the Holy Spirit.

Paul was diametrically opposed to parading one's own ability in lieu of the Holy Spirit. Perhaps you will recall the following words of Paul:

> When I came to you, brothers, I did not come with eloquence or superior wisdom as I proclaimed to you the testimony about God. For I resolved to know nothing while I was with you except Jesus Christ and him crucified. I came to you in weakness and fear, and with much trembling. My message and my preaching were not with wise and persuasive words, but with a demonstration of the Spirit's power (1 Cor. 2:1-4).

Yet, today our message is in evidence of showmanship and state of the art technology. Paul, on the other hand, was convinced that the Holy Spirit would confirm his words. But today, modern Christians are convinced that finesse, flanked by state of the art technology, will draw the lost to Christ. Indeed, it is a marvel to most Christians today that the Church exploded in the New Testament without fabulous church buildings, polished performances, and the 20th century technology that has spawned the perfection of these and other devices relied on today.

An Inferior Substitute

However, all these carnal things in our high tech world are inferior to the Holy Spirit by all means, and cannot possibly act as a substitute. Sophistication, at its best, will only cause church growth. This only means that the church organization will experience an increase in membership by drawing church members from one church to another.

The Holy Spirit accomplished far more. He can bring revival, and with it all the phenomenon seen at Azusa Street at the turn of the century. Revival results in church growth through conversions, but also in much, much more! Holy Spirit-sparked revival brings the power of God to deliver drug addicts from drugs and alcoholics from alcohol. It also repairs broken marriages and brings healing to the sick.

Today we offer very little supernatural deliverance for anything; instead we offer the nicest church in town. Many Pentecostal preachers can't pray for the sick (not with any hope of seeing them healed, anyway) or deliver alcoholics or drug addicts from the chemicals that bind them. For these difficulties, for failing marriages, and for just about anything else, we offer counseling. People drawn to the church for this "nicest church in town" ambiance invariably end up as weak Christians.

Those who find Christ in less than powerful ways and end up in churches like this develop a very shallow reference point: how nice the church is and how smoothly it operates. They have no recollection of how exciting it is to meet with God or attend a church where the Holy Spirit is in command and there's no tell-ing what may happen next. The kind of "nice" reference point Christians are developing in our movement could very well make us as rigidly denominational as any Lutheran or Presbyterian church.

Judge for yourself what glorifies God most. Is God glori-fied most by a polished, well-oiled church machine, or by strong families with drug-free teens and stable marriages?

A.W. Tozer once said, "The Great Commission is not the first call to the Church." Such a statement shocks many whose lives are consumed with fine-tuning their churches to draw in new members, but I must agree with Tozer. Tozer reminds us that Jesus first told His disciples to go to Jerusalem and tarry there until they were endued with power from on high. Tozer concludes that Jesus had no desire for them to do the work of God until they had a powerful encounter with Him.

The disciples were very much like second generation Chris-tians. They had already been living with Jesus for the past three years. Christianity was already a way of life for them. Jesus real-ized that they needed a power encounter before they could carry out the work God had for them.

"Do I Now Please God or Man?"

Sophistication develops what I term "efficiency," a philoso-phy overstating the importance of doing things right. Under this philosophy, every church building has to be built "right." It must be the most opulent place of worship in town, featuring state of the art sound systems, the latest in stain-guard carpeting, and the best padded pews. It must be an architectural marvel. Similarly, the ministry of that church must resemble the best the world has to offer. Each individual involved must rival the latest secular entertainer.

The rallying cry of the church has become, "Come on! Let's do it right! We'll prove to that evil world that we can put on a show every bit as good as theirs." In its mad dash to employ 20th century technology to further the cause of Christ, the church has become consumed with emulating the style and showmanship that accompanies this technology in the secular world. The secular media has attempted to be as crowd pleasing as possible, and the church has followed its lead. The soothing, entertaining services that result are seldom offensive, so they frequently draw people to the church organization.

On the other hand, the Holy Spirit is effective not just efficient. *While efficiency strives to do things right, effectiveness strives to do right things.* Right things are those which concern God most. God is concerned most about delivering unsaved people from the wages of their sin no matter what it takes. That means we cannot compromise and may even — Oh, no! Not that! — offend some people.

Sophistication and its companion, efficiency, lead us to do the work of God in the most inoffensive way, which often results in compromise. No one's going to be offended by one of our services, no sir! Why, that might impair the numerical growth of the church. Instead, we can now present all that the Bible says in such a way that every visitor will find the church to be a fun, comfortable place to be because it does things right.

If all we are drawing people to is an organization, then the organization must continually change (compromise) to keep everybody happy. Strong standards must come down because the morals of this world are coming down.

Standard-Setters or Trendsetters?

God never called the church to be a trendsetter. The church should be a moral-setter instead. However, today, instead of us affecting the trends of the world by maintaining high standards, these same trends are dictating our standards. If you're intent on being an "in" Christian, you wouldn't be caught dead in anything but the latest fashion.

I'm not against nice clothes, but I am adamantly opposed to fashion that countermands our morals. We have allowed a worldly spirit to influence us because of our great need for sophistication that is wholly incompatible with practical Christianity. I was once talking to an ex-prostitute who had gotten saved. She was excitedly telling me about all the things God had been teaching her. To my initial surprise, one of these things was fashion. She said that the Lord was teaching her what clothing she should wear and shouldn't wear. I couldn't help asking what she thought about the fashion statement the church is making.

"I see 'Christian' women dressed like prostitutes all too often," she replied. "I see women in the church wearing clothes on Sunday morning designed to arouse men, clothes that the Holy Spirit has told me never to wear again now that I represent Jesus Christ." How is it that a former prostitute can see this but the church can't?

I'm sure many of you remember when the mini-skirt was popular in the late 1960s and early 1970s. Do you know when that fashion ceased to be "in" with teenage girls? The mini-skirt went out when moms began wearing them. When I was in high school, mini-skirts weren't the only fad. There was also a more dangerous fad: marijuana. Do you know when teens began using more powerful drugs? It was when dad began smoking joints. When the moral-setters lower their standards, their moral subordinates lower their standards even more.

This is especially true when we consider the Church of Jesus Christ. We, the Church, are supposed to be the number one moral-setters on this planet. When we lower our standards, the world drops its standards also, becoming even worse. Because the church is continually lowering its standards, it is now faced with problems that should not arise in God's house.

A House of Prayer?

Whenever the church lacks discernment, it has a problem calling sin, "sin." We are dealing more with marriage counseling today than ever before. Why? We say that it is simply because there are more marriages falling apart today. But why are they falling apart? They're falling apart because we are afraid to preach on the sin of divorce for fear of offending the many divorced and remarried people in our churches.

Then he entered the temple area and began driving out those who were selling. "It is written," he said to them, 'My house will be a house of prayer' ; but you have made it 'a den of robbers' " (Luke 19:45-46).

When Jesus says, "My house will be a house of prayer," He is making prayer pre-eminent. He is saying that prayer should stand over and above all other things in the house of God. If prayer is not first and foremost, we lose our ability to discern. Jesus went on to say that when those in God's house don't pray, they rob God. It becomes a den of thieves.

Mindful of how the money-changers in the temple were "evicted" by Jesus, we in Christianity have sought (unsuccessfully) to keep money-changers out of the church.

However, there was nothing wrong with the money-changers being there. The problem with them was that they had become thieves. Yet, that was not the greatest problem. The greatest problem was that they had become thieves and nobody noticed! They didn't notice because they had lost their discernment, and they had lost their discernment because they were not praying.

Jesus was really getting to the root of their problem when He highlighted the point that God's house is to be first of all a house of prayer.

The lack of discernment has never been more evident than it is today. Why else would the national news media need to call attention to the sins of the church? Shouldn't the church see these things before the world does? When the church does see these things first, it is frequently the laity who are seeing them before the clergy. Why does it take a national scandal to cause us to take action? It is because our prayerlessness has blinded us to our own sins.

Wouldn't it be wonderful for pastors to realize that the church can raise the morals of the world by maintaining their own high standards instead of trying to counter the worlds standards through some kind of "Christian" pseudo?

In the New Testament

After we had been there a number of days, a prophet named Agabus came down from Judea. Coming over to us, he took Paul's belt, tied his own hands and feet with it and said, "The Holy Spirit says, 'In this way the Jews of Jerusalem will bind the owner of this belt and will hand him over to the Gentiles' " (Acts 21:10-11).

Paul was warned that he would be severely persecuted during his upcoming trip to Jerusalem, but he went anyway and was persecuted just as Agabus had prophesied. Just as a mob of enraged Jews were beating him, Paul was rescued and arrested by a group of Roman soldiers and officers intent on quieting the uproar. Shortly after, Paul was allowed to defend himself in front of all the people. It was a perfect opportunity for him to present the gospel in a "less offensive" way. A small compromise, a few ambiguous phrases, and some carefully chosen words could have made Paul the most popular fellow in town.

However, Paul chose another course of action. In Acts 22 he told the crowd about his power encounter with Christ. He did this because he wanted the people to find Christ in the same dynamic way he had (the only way to find Christ, as far as Paul was concerned). This didn't gain any popularity for him or for the church. Paul no more than got the final words of his testimony out when the crowd roared, "Rid the earth of him! He's not fit to live!"

Today, we could really teach the poor befuddled Apostle a lesson. We realize that he really blew it! He must have known that while his testimony had great potential to lead at least some in the crowd to Christ, it had equal potential to offend many in the crowd. It would have been more profitable for him to discuss something like God's great love for the Jewish people. After all, that would have been true; God does love the Jews. Such a smooth presentation would have established very good relations between Paul and the Jews, and wouldn't they be more likely to listen to someone they liked?

That's the typical modern argument. However, unlike most Christians today, Paul was not concerned with doing things right, the way that guarantees popularity and applause. Paul was concerned about doing right things, the things that please God. He knew God wanted people to meet Him in a powerful way and would not do anything to jeopardize that.

In the Old Testament

Now Naaman was commander of the army of the king of Aram. He was a great man in the sight of his master and highly regarded, because through him the Lord had given victory to Aram. He was a valiant soldier, but he had leprosy. Now bands from Aram had gone out and had taken captive a young girl from Israel, and she served Naaman's wife. She said to her mistress, "If only my master would see the prophet who is in Samaria! He would cure him of his leprosy." Naaman went to his master and told him what the girl from Israel had said. "By all means, go," the king of Aram replied. "I will send a letter to the king of Israel." So Naaman left, taking with him ten talents of silver, six thousand shekels of gold and ten sets of clothing. The letter that he took to the king of Israel read: "With this letter I am sending my servant Naaman to you so that you may cure him of his leprosy." As soon as the king of Israel read the letter, he tore his robes and said, "Am I God? Can I kill and bring back to life? Why does this fellow send someone to me to be cured of his leprosy? See how he is trying to pick a quarrel with me!" When Elisha the man of God heard that the king of Israel had torn his robes, he sent him this message: "Why have you torn your robes? Have the man come to me and he will know that there is a prophet in Israel." So Naaman went with his horses and chariots

and stopped at the door of Elisha's house. Elisha sent a
messenger to say to him, "Go, wash yourself seven
times in the Jordan, and your flesh will be restored and
you will be cleansed." But Naaman went away angry
and said, "I thought that he would surely come out to
me and stand and call on the name of the Lord his God,
wave his hand over the spot and cure me of my leprosy
(2 Kings 5:1-11).

Today's Christian could set these ancient, well-meaning but
ignorant people from the Bible straight. Observe that the anointed
one, the prophet of God, would not come out of his house to
greet this man that the Scriptures called "highly esteemed." We
latter-day Christians would know better than to pull such a stunt.
Today's "prophet" would not only come out of the house, he would
have network and local news teams there to cover the event so
that he could humbly do the work of God.

The great war hero Naaman was expecting to have his pride
stroked. He thought there should be great fanfare. He thought the
prophet himself should have come out, not just a messenger.
Where was the great hoopla that followed a celebrity? To make
matters worse, Elisha relayed a very belittling instruction to
Naaman: he told him to dip himself in the river seven times.
Naaman was expecting something spectacular (perhaps the voice
of the archangel and the trumpet of God).

Of course Elisha was right in what he did. He had something most of us don't have today: he had direct contact with
God regularly. He had more to base his actions on than a sermon
or a set of general rules taken from the Scriptures. He had the
very heartbeat of God on which to base his actions. This is how
the prophet knew that God wanted to deal not only with the leprosy of Naaman, but also with his pride. Therefore, Elisha would
not come out of his house and thus fuel the fire of Naaman's
pride. This is also why he gave him such humbling instructions.

Our current approach, the "right thing to do" in the eyes of men, would have allowed Naaman to wallow in his pride. In fact, it would have swelled his head even more. When we do things right instead of doing right things, we never force men to humble themselves before God. We in fact, nurture their pride. Pride keeps men from coming to God. That's the result of doing things our way, the "right" way.

Sophistication is Not the Problem

By now, I'm sure that many of you think this author is against everything and hungering for a return to the Stone Age, where there's no refinement to infect the body of Christ. This is just not the case. I'm not against the use of our world's technology in the spreading of the gospel. I believe our ever-increasing technology can become the greatest tool for spreading the gospel Christians have ever had. I'm not against the church being a well-polished organization, either. If we're even going to bother doing something that will represent God to our community, we should do it as well as we can. I'm just against one thing: replacing the Holy Spirit. The whole thrust of the Pentecostal movement has been the baptism of the Holy Spirit and helping people find Christ in a powerful way. When anything replaces that, we no longer serve God's purpose in His kingdom.

One of my greatest fears is that we will no longer hear from God. In that unfortunate event, God will be forced to raise up another movement, one through which He can manifest himself in a powerful way. This has happened time and time again. God raises up a movement flowing in God's Spirit, seeing His signs and wonders. Then that movement becomes more and more formal to gain the respect of the community. That movement ends up an ecclesiastical "stuffed shirt," unwilling to move in the Spirit and see God's miracles. Then, God raises a different group who will.

A Proper Perspective

I remember reading E.M. Bounds once where he stated, "God will not anoint technology. He will not anoint machinery. He will not anoint programs. God anoints men and women who pray." What the church needs today more than programs or state of the art technology is saints who will pray; without them we are doomed to failure. With saints who pray, the power will be restored to our gospel. We will no longer have men and women attending our churches who are bound by life controlling sin. We will have men and women anointed by God who will know how to pull down strongholds and cast down imaginations.

Particularly, our preachers must be men of prayer. I would much rather be a powerful preacher than a polished pastor, not coming to you with eloquence or wisdom, not coming to you with learned oratory skills, but rather in evidence of the Spirit and power of God. This should be a must for any man who calls himself a Pentecostal preacher.

Chapter V

Rebuilding the Ancient Boundaries

The neglect of prayer is a grand hindrance to holiness. — John Wesley, founder of the Methodist Church

Have you ever seen anyone pray as much as the victim of some tragedy? The Christian family which has lost its home to a hurricane or tornado, the saint enduring the death of a loved one, the newlyweds who are struck down economically by sudden, unexpected unemployment — they all run desperately to their unchanging, all-knowing Father.

Hard times have a way of drawing us to God. When we experience loss, we realize there is one thing we have which we cannot lose — our relationship with God. In our pain, it is to Him we turn in prayer. In prayer alone can we wrap ourselves securely in His love and experience His peace to ease our hurts and alleviate our fears. Finally, the stabbing pain of loss caused by the death of a loved one is soothed by the Holy Spirit. All the damage done by the violent storm is repaired as God provides. The

Lord graciously and miraculously provides work, and economic security sets in. Life is back to "normal" again.

Then, as the good times begin to roll, prayer becomes as much a memory as the disaster that initiated it. As time marches on, hard times set in again from the lack of seeking God. With a renewed attitude of dependence, we return to seeking Him. The Lord hears our prayers and delivers us from our troubles (again); then when times are good, we stop seeking Him (again). Most of us seem to run through this cycle in our lives. As long as we're enjoying a life of ease, we fail to commune with our God, but the moment we're in a jam, we rush to confer with Him. This cycle repeats itself in our lives with varying frequency. It may occur weekly, monthly, or yearly. When dealing with the church on the whole, however, the cycle generally repeats itself about once every three generations. The most harmful result of this cycle is that during large segments of it we do not pray.

The Ancient Boundaries

This cycle is nothing new. It marred man's relationship with God throughout the Old Testament, as Nehemiah described in the following prayer:

> But they were disobedient and rebelled against you, they put your law behind their backs. They killed your prophets, who admonished them in order to turn them back to you; they committed awful blasphemies. So you handed them over to their enemies, who oppressed them. But when they were oppressed, they cried out to you. From heaven you heard them, and in your great compassion you gave them deliverers, who rescued them from the hand of their enemies.
>
> But as soon as they were at rest, they again did what was evil in your sight. Then you abandoned them to the hand of their enemies so that they ruled over them. And when they cried out to you again, you heard from heaven, and in your compassion you

delivered them time after time.

You warned them to return to your law, but they
became arrogant and disobeyed your commands. They
sinned against your ordinances, by which a man will
live if he obeys them. Stubbornly they turned their backs
on you, became stiff-necked and refused to listen. For
many years you were patient with them. By your Spirit,
you admonished them through your prophets. Yet they
paid no attention, so you handed them over to the neigh-
boring peoples. But in your great mercy, you did not
put an end to them or abandon them, for you are a gra-
cious and merciful God (Neh. 9:26-31).

As far back as 2,400 years ago, Nehemiah was dealing with
the same problem: God's people seek Him in hard times and neglect Him in good times. As a result of the people's rejection of
the Lord in the good times, hard times set in. In this instance, the
ancient Jews' rejection of Him led to the Assyrian captivity of
the northern kingdom of Israel and the subsequent takeover of
the southern kingdom of Judah by the Babylonians. Jerusalem
was destroyed, and its remaining inhabitants were carried away
by their conquerors. However, after the people began seeking
God again, their captors allowed some of them to return to their
homeland, though still a conquered people.

In the account above, we find that under Nehemiah's lead-
ership the returned exiles had just finished rebuilding the walls
that encompassed Jerusalem. Those walls represented more to
those people at that time than walls around our homes would
mean to us today. At that time and place they represented the
boundaries in which the residents of the city agreed to live. They
weren't imprisoned within these walls, but it was customary for
anyone wanting to be identified as a Jerusalemite to live within
what these boundaries represented. They represented a certain
lifestyle which was to be maintained regardless of where they
were.

Boundaries Today

Today we don't have physical boundaries we are subject to, but we are to have boundaries: moral, spiritual boundaries. These boundaries identify us as citizens of the kingdom of God, even as the walls of Jerusalem identified citizens of Jerusalem. In past years we Christians were clearly distinguished by (and sometimes scorned for) the boundaries we chose to maintain.

Yet today we have moved our boundaries in spite of clear scriptural admonishment to the contrary.

> Do not move the ancient boundaries established by your fathers (Prov. 22:28).

In our world, Christians indulge in the same ungodly activities as non-Christians to the point that a believer cannot be distinguished from an unbeliever. Popular theology dictates that we Christians can do anything and God will bless it simply because we are Christians. Life in the church is allegedly non-stop party time. Celebration is the catchword for most Christians. In short, we live in a church without boundaries or limits, and such a church is doomed.

The most common defense for removing the ancient boundaries is that to maintain them could mean a legalistic lifestyle in this, the day of grace. But the fact that we live under grace today does not mean that we should have no limits to our activities. *What boundaries were to those living under legalism, conviction becomes to the person living under grace.*

But before we can begin to explore remedies that will restore our boundaries, we must first understand how they were erected.

How Boundaries Are Established

Boundaries are established by conviction. The root of the problem is that today's church has no convictions. It is because of this that the church has no boundaries which, in turn, leads every person to do whatever he feels like. The next logical question, "So then how are convictions established?" can be explained in Jesus' own words:

> But I tell you the truth: It is good for you that I am going away. Unless I go away, the Counselor will not come to you; but if I go, I will send Him to you. When He comes, He will convict the world of guilt in regard to sin and righteousness, because I am going to the Father where you can see me no longer (John 16:7-10).

Clearly, convictions are established by the Holy Spirit. The Holy Spirit convicts in three areas: in sin, in righteousness, and in judgment. We need to give good thought to the area of righteousness. Today there is very little righteous living. If the Holy Spirit is to convict us of righteousness, why aren't more people convicted of it? Has the Holy Spirit taken a vacation or gone out on strike? No, of course not. But we have, judging by our woefully inconsistent prayer lives. Where there is no prayer, there is no Holy Spirit to convict.

Usually we end up trying to base our actions on the Word of God. You can base your convictions on the Bible, but only if you are a person of prayer. If you aren't a person of prayer, you will not have the guidance and instruction from the Holy Spirit that you need. God never intended for the Bible to be used without His Spirit. Without the Holy Spirit, we can twist the Bible to condone anything we want. I have spoken to people who have justified their rock music, their dancing, and even their drinking through the Bible.

The Scriptures have never been a source of conviction apart from the Holy Spirit. The New Testament Pharisees are ample proof of this. They knew and could quote all the Old Testament Scriptures, but that knowledge was useless to them because they had a wrong spirit. With their knowledge of the Old Testament, they were able to crucify the Son of God. This is why Jesus said it was to our advantage that He leave. He wanted to send the

Helper. Without the Helper, we could have ended up no better than the Pharisees.

Jesus basically said, "I am giving you the Helper so that, among other things, He will convict you of righteousness." Then He said that the reason the Holy Spirit needs to convict us of righteousness is that He (Jesus) was going to the Father and would not be with us anymore. Since He would not be with us anymore, we would need a Helper to remind us of what He was like. The Holy Spirit convicts us of righteousness by reminding us of what Jesus was like.

In addition, Christ is our righteousness. When we have no prayer life, we lose a sense of the righteousness of Christ. We begin to do things that Christ would never do, choosing quite on our own what sin is or isn't. We couldn't be more wrong. It's not up to us to determine what is sin. That's up to the Holy Spirit. Our life before we became Christians does not determine what we will or will not be convicted about, either. The Helper is to decide this.

I have heard people say, "Just because I am in the world doesn't mean I am of the world. Just because I am doing things the world does doesn't mean I am of the world." This, too, is a great deception.

Please do not misunderstand our purpose as Christians. Our purpose is not just to figure out what is sinful and what is not. Our primary goal is not to see how much we can get away with, or to see how close we can get to the world and still hang on to our salvation. Our number one purpose is to see how close we can get to God, not how close we can get to the world. The only way to get close to the Lord is in prayer where the Holy Spirit can reveal to us what pleases God and what doesn't. There are no easy shortcuts. That's the only way.

Today it is popular to base our convictions on whether or not there's a chapter and verse that forbids a given activity. We are then left indulging in any activity for which there is not a corresponding biblical "Thou shalt not." This is very far from true conviction which is determined by the Holy Spirit speaking to us, often telling us to abstain from an activity because it is a weight that hinders us from running the race set before us, not because that activity is a sin. However, if we don't pray, we'll never have that inner sense of what pleases God and what doesn't.

Prayer Develops Conviction

With an understanding of how convictions are developed, we gain an understanding of how convictions are curtailed. Simply put, if convictions are born out of prayer, they can be killed by prayerlessness.

That's just what happens to most moves of God. The founders of any movement are pillars of prayer. The first generation of any move of God are people of prayer. They have nothing but God. They have no beautiful buildings or fine sound systems. They simply have God. Therefore, they must pray. When God begins something, He does it by giving someone some type of revelation or vision. God usually begins with an individual because the masses of people will not respond very quickly. That individual or handful of believers have this great vision before them, and yet they recognize their own limitations and inabilities. Therefore, they pray that the path God has called them to will be established. Because of their dependency on prayer, they begin to develop convictions which become the boundaries for that movement.

The first generation always establishes the boundaries for their Christian movement. It is very important to realize that the boundaries they set up are based on what would keep them on the path (vision) that God called them to. Their convictions are not based upon sin or the lack of it. Their convictions (boundaries) are determined by whether or not an activity helps them to stay on the path God wants them on. Often, it has very little to do with whether or not an activity is specifically denounced as sinful in the Bible. The entire matter is determined by whether that activity would sidetrack them or not.

Their continual prayer and trust in the Lord results in

blessings for them and their churches. However. as we discussed earlier, their children are not taught the importance of prayer. To make matters worse, because of the material blessings granted to their parents and their churches, these children are seldom drawn to prayer. They have fabulous church facilities and can end up relying on them and not God.

Conviction Becomes Tradition

The Scriptures indicate that God will bless the seed of those who delight in Him:

> "Praise the Lord. Blessed is the man who fears the Lord, who finds great delight in his commands. *His children will be mighty in the land*; the generation of the upright will be blessed" (Ps. 112:1-2, emphasis added).

The first generation prays and subsequently finds great delight in God. This brings blessings for their children. Remember the cycle? Once we are blessed, we tend to stop praying.

Without prayer, these children do not develop deeply entrenched, Holy-Ghost-wrought conviction, but they do try to live within the boundaries set by their parents. For the most part, however, they do this to keep tradition ("This is the way Mom and Dad always said it was" or "This is the way it's always been"), not because they are moving at the stirring direction of the Holy Spirit. Hence, what was conviction to the first generation (because of prayer) becomes simple tradition to the second (because of prayerlessness).

Tradition Becomes a Waste of Time

The third generation surfaces and sees this for what it is: legalism. Following rules and laws without conviction is nothing less than legalism. These new Christians see no purpose in abstaining from something "just because that's the way it's always been." But without prayer, they're in no position to develop any convictions more genuine than those legalistic traditions of their parents.

From lack of prayer (and, subsequently, conviction), the third generation bases their activities on what is or is not sin. Their mentality is, "If you can't find a Bible verse prohibiting it, then it must be okay to do." They fail to realize that their forefathers based their activities on what would keep them on the path God called them to. The whole thought of following the ancient ways is lost.

Without Purpose

Without prayer, we lose our reason for being. We live our Christian lives with one rather ignoble purpose: to escape hell. Such a person, who is a Christian with that solitary mission, will base his entire life's conduct on whether something is prohibited as sinful or not in the Scriptures.

This can best be illustrated by comparing it to a wedding night. Imagine that it's my wedding night. My bride and I are having a romantic candle-lit dinner. I reach across the table, take both of her hands in mine, and say, "Lou Ann, I love you, and I want you to know that no matter how many other women I may be seeing on the side, I'll always love you. In fact, while we're on the subject, just how many affairs can I have with other women before you'll divorce me? I mean, believe me, divorce is the last thing on my mind. It's just that I don't want to stay tied down to one woman, that's all."

Isn't that what we are doing when we base our convictions on what is and is not blatant sin? It's essentially saying, "God, I love you, and I really don't want to go to hell. Lord, while we're on the subject, just how much can I get away with and still make it into heaven?"

What do you think the reactions would be to such statements? My wife's response to my hypothetical statement on our hypothetical wedding night would probably be something like, "I thought you were interested in doing all you could to make our relationship even more beautiful than it is now, not just keep it in existence!" I think Jesus would have a similar response. He would likely say, "I thought you'd be most concerned with seeing how close you could come to me, not how far away you could get."

The Dilemma Today

The prophet Jeremiah painted a vivid picture of the dilemma facing the church today. Notice the prophet's call and the response of the people to it:

> This is what the Lord says: "Stand at the cross-roads and look; ask for the ancient paths, ask where the good way is, and walk in it, and you will find rest for your souls. But you said, 'We will not walk in it.' I appointed watchmen over you and said, 'Listen to the sound of the trumpet!' But you said, 'We will not listen'" (Jer. 6;16-17).

Today, because of prayerlessness, the strong standard of righteous living is hard to find in most of our churches. The ancient boundaries have been forsaken. The result is a chaotic, confused church left to its own resources to establish its convictions, consumed with debating what is and is not sin. The only guide left is the Bible which is a very weak guide with no interpreter. Others almost forsake the Bible and insist that all convictions are relative to one's pre-Christian life. Most of these have flocked to nearly every entertainment medium conceivable under the heretical rallying cry, "Satan has had the good entertainment long enough! It's time for Christians to enjoy it for a while."

A Solemn Assembly

We must get back to prayer, allowing the Holy Spirit to instill immovable conviction and rebuild the ancient boundaries. If we fail to, we are doomed as a movement. If we fail to, we have seen our best days spiritually. Without praying moms and dads, relentlessly pursuing God, we will raise a generation of children who do not know God. These children will have the same attitude toward sin as the prostitute in Proverbs who wipes her mouth and states, "I have done no wrong" (Prov. 30:20).

The church today is an explosion of celebration. The model Christian life is a showcase of ease and fellowship gatherings. The words "fun, food, and fellowship" are considered to be the high point of every church bulletin. What the church really needs today is a solemn assembly, an assembly where our sorrow for our sinfulness can be expressed. Nehemiah and his people held just such an assembly. There was celebration, but the celebration was capped off with introspection.

> On the twenty-fourth day of the same month, the Israelites gathered together, fasting and wearing sackcloth and having dust on their heads. Those of the Israelite descent had separated themselves from all foreigners. They stood in their places and confessed their sins and the wickedness of their fathers. They stood where they were and read from the Book of the Law of the Lord in a fourth of the day, and spent another fourth in confession and in worshipping the Lord their God (Neh. 9:1-3).

Our modern day church needs a solemn assembly. We don't need another celebration; we need our God. The Lord wants to search our hearts. He wants a church without spot or wrinkle.

What are your convictions? Are they based on the direction of the Holy Spirit? Or are they based on your convenience? Or are they based on legalism? Consider these matters in your heart and spend time on your knees consulting the Lord about them. In an effort to make sure that the walls of Jerusalem were not torn down again, Nehemiah found it necessary for the people of God to invest some time in prayer, fasting, and confession. Times haven't really changed that much. That's what we need today just as badly.

I'm not saying that we should go back and do things the way they used to be done just because that's the way things were done in "the good ol' days." If we do that, we end up back in legalism. All I'm saying is that we must get back to prayer. Then we must allow the Holy Spirit to instill within us conviction that will guide us into a lifestyle that pleases God.

I'm also not saying that the third generation is destined to lose out with God. They are simply victims of the cycle we go through. But that cycle can be broken! I feel one of the most important things we can do is to teach our children to pray. We must teach them to pray based on their need for God. We must teach them that they need to pray no matter how their lives are going. Even if they are the most blessed people on earth, they need to pray. Moms and dads, the best way to teach your children to pray is to be people of prayer yourselves. The most effective prayer teachers for them are you! Remember that the biggest reason most children know nothing about prayer today is because Mom and Dad have stopped praying.

God wants to build first generation believers. Regardless of where you stand chronologically in your Christian heritage, you can become a first generation believer if you're willing to develop your prayer life. First generation Christians are simply Christians who pray.

Chapter VI

Counterculture

I remember your ancient laws, O Lord, and I find comfort in them (Ps. 119:52).

David found comfort in the ancient laws of God. King David must have really been out of touch. Today we know that the ancient laws of God are quite outdated. Today we have tuned-in to the "new thing" God is doing. The old way of approaching God through repentance and the contrite heart is considered out of touch. Today we gleefully approach God. We laugh in the face of repentance.

I'm being a bit facetious and at the same time trying to address a problem in the church. The problem is that we have abandoned the ancient laws of God through allowing a rather rebellious frame of mind to lead us into a misunderstanding of the character and nature of God.

Consider what the ancient laws really are. The word "laws" in this verse is translated, "judgments or customs." Judgments are the decisions by which a custom is established. The judgments of God are the decisions He has made in order to establish the customs, or the way of life, for the people of God. In some societies the customs (laws) are so strict, and ingrained that to break one would mean certain death. Many of our states still use capital punishment as the form of judgment for breaking certain laws or customs. Typically, people are very cultural, and when someone breaks away from the accepted customs of the day, there tends to be a revolution.

Jesus was a revolutionary! He was a counterculturalist. That which ultimately sent Christ to the Cross was his counterculture views of the accepted religious society. Jesus came to a group of legalistic religious leaders and told them that the "new thing" is called "grace," and that the old way was dead.

> For we have heard him say that this Jesus of Nazareth will destroy this place and change the customs Moses handed down to us (Acts 6:14).

Jesus changed the customs of Moses. That's revolutionary! The difference between Jesus and all other counterculturalists is that He introduced us to the one true culture, the culture of the Cross. Most other customs or cultures are man-made. From His day on, the Cross was to be the center of all things. The Cross represents self-sacrifice. It represents the crucified life.

A Change in the Priesthood

Look at what God says about a change of the priesthood. In Hebrews 7:12 we read, "For when there is a change of the priesthood, there must also be a change of the law." This of course is a reference to Jesus. The writer of Hebrews goes on to say, "For it is declared: "You are a priest forever, in the order of Melchizedek." The former regulation is set aside because it was weak and useless (for the law made nothing perfect), and a better hope is introduced, by which we draw near to God" (Heb. 7:17-19). Jesus set aside the former regulation, the custom of Moses, to introduce us to a new culture. The culture of the Cross. It is through the culture of the Cross that we can now draw near to God.

Different Cultures

I once had an opportunity to go to Seoul, Korea. While I was there I went to a restaurant. After I had finished eating I was looking for the rest room but could not find a door that looked like it might be the right one (I couldn't read their language). After a while I saw a man walk into a room and come out in a relatively short time. Then I saw another man enter and exit shortly after that. I decided that that must be the door to the rest room. About the time I was getting up to use the facility I saw a woman come out of the same room. This totally confused and shocked me. Then I was made aware that it was a part of their culture for men and women to use the same facility at the same time. The reason it shocked me was because in our society (the United States) you would never think of doing that. It was not shocking at all to the Koreans because it is a part of their accepted culture.

Sometime after this experience I heard a news report on the radio in America that totally shocked me. It was about the growing trend of cross-dressers. A cross-dresser is someone who wears the clothing of the opposite sex. The news report was how one city was being forced to provide special rest rooms for cross-dressers in public buildings. It stated that it would be discriminatory to not provide them with their own facilities.

Why is that so shocking to the average conservative? It's because cross-dressing is countercultural. "A woman must not wear men's clothing, nor a man wear women's clothing, for the Lord your God detests anyone who does this" (Deut. 22:5).

It may seem like a small issue but in reality it is symptomatic of a much larger issue. In our society men and women have separate public rest rooms. A cross-dresser cannot enter the men's room dressed as a woman. He also cannot enter the woman's room because he is not a woman though he is dressed like one. To accept the idea of providing them with their own facilities goes against the Word of God but it also goes contrary to what we have stood for as a nation for all these generations.

Revolution

In the 1960s America experienced a revolution which resulted in establishing a drug culture that has dominated liberal thinkers for over 30 years. This counterculture has done much to destroy the moral fiber of our country. Liberal thinkers feel that they are open-minded. They seem to believe conservative thinkers are very narrow. It's possible that in reality, liberal thinkers are simply willing to break tradition and conservatives want to maintain tradition. When it comes to man-made tradition, one is probably not much more "right" than the other. If however, maintaining tradition means guarding what we consider purity of doctrine and the Word of God, that is another issue.

Current Dilemma

When we consider the current dilemma the church in America faces we see a very interesting similarity. The church was also affected by this revolution. It resulted in the Jesus People movement which was closely followed by the Charismatic movement. Both of these movements were birthed in the 1960s. Both of them were very countercultural compared to the standard the church had accepted for many decades. The Jesus People movement introduced what has become known as Christian rock and roll music. The Charismatic movement, in large measure, convinced us that worldliness is acceptable which has climaxed with the Health, Wealth, and Prosperity (Faith) movement.

I remember reading articles in the early 1970s by Charismatic leaders talking about how legalistic the old Pentecostal movement had become. They espoused a freedom that had no boundaries whatsoever. With time we found our own people doing things they would never have even discussed prior to that. Things like going to movies or dances or even bars and nightclubs were simply things we didn't do. It's very possible that some Pentecostal people had become legalistic about these things, however, the acceptance of worldliness is not the proper way to counter legalism.

The Charismatic movement as a whole has lacked good solid

theology. Often they (the Charismatics) found themselves still attending their mainline denominational church even after they were saved. This kept feeding them a very liberal (worldly) theology even after they had accepted Christ as their Saviour. A liberal theology typically abuses grace.

Liberal vs. Conservative

Typically the Charismatics are far more liberal, while the Pentecostals are more conservative. One of the reasons for this is that the Pentecostal movement has more history (short as it may be) than the Charismatic movement. However, maintaining any movement's history really should not be the primary issue. The issue should be that of maintaining the culture Jesus introduced us to within the pages of Scripture.

Within the church, conservatives and liberals are beginning to clash. Is it possible that after three decades of an anti-Cross culture the conservatives are going to rise up and say, "We have had enough! We don't like what our churches have become. We don't like the fact that there are as many affairs going on in the church as there are in the world. We are tired of finding out that our children drink, dance, and rock-and-roll. We are tired of feeling pressured into being trendy. We are tired of being pastored by men whose egos are bigger than their God, who have no anointing, and who do not pray."

Conservatives believe sin should be dealt with and people should conform to the culture Jesus introduced us to. Liberals tend to accommodate sin and attempt to adjust the church to make it more relevant so as to fit the lifestyle of those who won't conform to Jesus. The conservative says, "You must make kids conform to Jesus." The liberal says, "Jesus needs to become what these kids need." Much of what the church espouses as church growth issues today is that of understanding our culture and conforming the church to it. The very thing that got Jesus in trouble with His peers is that he would not conform to their traditions.

We are not to accept things based on the current culture. We are to compare the current culture to the one true culture set forth in the Scriptures. How would we justify this trend of accommodating current trends to God's statement of himself, "I the Lord do not change" (Mal. 3:6). Consider Matthew 18:3, "And he said: 'I tell you the truth, unless you change and become like little children, you will never enter the kingdom of heaven.'" The Scriptures tell us over and over that we are the ones who must change. The current anti-Cross counterculture believes that unless the church changes and becomes relevant it can no longer reach people today.

What if the Bible is right? What if God actually means what he says? What is going to happen to most of the worldly church today if James is telling the truth when he says, "Anyone who chooses to be a friend of the world becomes an enemy of God" (James 4:4).

Attention Getters

Who are the people that get the most attention in any society? The liberals! The liberals get the attention because they have an agenda of change. Subsequently they tend to eventually gain control of the media. Within the church we see this also. The more liberal-minded ones control most of the television programs and popular magazines within the Charismatic/Pentecostal movement. They must draw attention to themselves to prove they are right.

Within all liberal attitudes is a thread of rebellion. This is often the case in the independent church, but not always. Many churches become independent because they reject authority. That rejection of authority can lead to deception. What you perceive to be God may not be God at all. Today it is common to belittle anything that has to do with denominations. Denominations represent authority. Granted, many mainline denominations have lost touch with God. However, they have lost touch because they left the message of the Cross, not because they became a denomination.

Rebellion always results in self-attention. Who are the teenagers we notice the most? It's the rebellious. The rebellious are the most trendy. They are always on the cutting edge. They are typically the most obvious ones in a crowd. Why don't the conservatives gain much attention? Typically it's because they live in submission. The "good" teenager obeys mom and dad. He dresses the way they suggest. He lives within the boundaries they establish. Subsequently he is looked upon as dull, narrow-minded, and out of touch, when in reality he simply lives in submission to his parents.

When the Bible addresses the issue of abandonment it always manifests itself through self-denial not self-glorification. Self-glorification comes many times simply through being the center of attention.

Worldliness

We need a proper definition of worldliness in order to better understand this. Worldliness is much more than doing the things the world does. Worldliness is basically bringing attention to self. Its root is pride. It is from pride that we desire to be exalted among men. Because of this desire to be exalted in the eyes of men, fashion becomes very important, becoming relevant to society then becomes the primary motivator.

How does the Cross differ from worldliness? It's really quite simple. Worldliness exalts man, while the Cross exalts God. Ultimately, Jesus was crucified because He revealed the idolatry in the hearts of others. That idol is self. True revival is that which restores a man's relationship with God. If there is any lifting up of man in what we would call a current move-of-God it does not fit into the true definition of revival.

The revival we refer to as "ours" is often called the Azusa Street revival. The current Pentecostal movement declares that the Holy Spirit ultimately swept through the entire country and world from this revival. Because we as a movement were birthed through a great "move of God," we have continued to seek for more "moves." The problem with seeking for a move of God is that we tend to lose a focus on repentance. Instead we pray for God to do something. You would be hard-pressed to find God moving in spite of men but rather because of men. The Azusa Street revival came as a result of men who were broken before God. Men were on their faces asking God to search their hearts. They were confessing sin, they were seeking God so that he might posses them to a greater degree. The result of their repentance was a sweep of the Spirit of God that changed history.

By comparison, the "revivals" in America's Charismatic/ Pentecostal churches today seem to lack integrity. Today there is a pressure to be a part of the "new thing" God is doing, and if you are not in it you are not with it. There exists today the same type of peer pressure I experienced in high school where in order to be seen as accepted by the other "cool" kids you had to do certain things and dress certain ways. Things that exalt man get all the press while the other things that are taking place in the kingdom of God get very little recognition.

In 1995 a sovereign move of God took place on several Evangelical Bible college campuses. These moves were marked by repentance and the public confession of sin. Students would go to chapel and not leave for several hours. The whole time they were praying for others, confessing their sin, and asking God to forgive them publicly. Some of the meetings lasted into the wee hours of the morning. Why didn't this get much attention? There were some articles printed about it but there was very little desire to get involved in these meetings. From my knowledge, very few pastors flew into these towns to get in on what was going on.

The Pentecostal movement in America has a rich history of prayer. We were a people that sought God. We had a hunger for God that drove us to our knees. Our prayers were not so much that God would continue the current move, but rather we wanted to be with God, we wanted God to shape us into His character, we wanted to walk in integrity. We were much more interested in God himself than speaking in tongues. Speaking in tongues was simply the result of our great hunger to be with God. Today we are seeking a move of God without repentance. We want an experience rather than God.

Repentance

What's wrong with repentance anyway? Repentance removes man's greatness. The desire to be great among men is what keeps a man from praying. I once attended a conference of evangelists. It was a conference that had much fanfare and lifted high the office of the evangelist. We talked a lot about our own greatness but very little about our God. Some would say that we talked about God by virtue of challenging people to get out there and save souls. The reality of it is that we want to do great things for God because of what it will do to exalt us in the eyes of men.

I was given the assignment of conducting the morning prayer meetings. This conference had about 200 evangelists registered, with around 600 people in attendance. The morning prayer meetings produced about three evangelists. Prayer and its importance was even preached about by those who did not come to the prayer meetings. What's wrong with prayer? It brings us to repentance and if we repent we cannot continue to pursue the things that exalt us rather than God.

There are many reports today of revival sweeping the nation. I want that as much as anybody does. However, I want God more than I want revival. If these "moves of God" are bringing people into repentance then I support them. If they simply become another place to go and sing until you can't sing anymore, I'm not interested. True revival will re-introduce the culture of the Cross to the church. If it's really revival we will gain a new sense of holiness. We will do away with the exaltation of man that we see in the "Christian" music industry. We won't want anything to do with men that are in the pulpit for personal gain rather than godliness. Revival will give us insight to the problems of the church. If the current "revivals" are not doing these things they will bear no serious fruit.

Chapter VII

The Fall of the Slight Tower

How the mighty have fallen. — King David, c. 1025 B.C.

Throughout the Old Testament, we read references to two different types of towers. The first of these is the "Strong Tower," one of God's many pseudonyms. Psalm 61:3 speaks of Him when it says, "You have been my refuge, a strong tower against the foe." This is just one of many such "Strong Tower" references which are laced throughout the Scriptures.

The second kind is the "slight tower," the type that was often erected for the keeper of a vineyard or for a flock. Its description as "slight" does not imply that it was either weak or flimsy. As we will see, these towers were, by definition, nearly impregnable by standards of that day. The prophet Isaiah speaks of it when he says, "He dug it up and cleared it of stones and planted it with the choicest vines. He built a watchtower in it" (Isa. 5:2). Other references to it are made in 2 Chronicles 26:10 and Micah 4:8.

Spiritually speaking, a slight tower is a refuge for the pastor (for whom the keeper of a vineyard is symbolic) or for the church (for whom the flock is symbolic). In our world, towers do not serve the same purposes or carry the same connotations that they did in the Old Testament. We'd be in error if we said that the Sears Tower in Chicago is just an overgrown biblical slight tower. *The International Bible Dictionary* helps us bridge this cultural gap with its description of biblical towers. It states, "Towers were erected not only on the outer walls and on the heights within the cities, but along the frontiers of a country, at points where the approach of an enemy could be decried at a distance (see Judg. 9:17, Isa. 21:6-9). A tower afforded refuge to the surrounding inhabitants in case of invasion; and often, when most of a city was subdued, the tower remained impregnable."

Our Strong Tower (the Lord) and the slight tower (the pastor, the church) both serve a similar function in that they are always to provide a refuge from the enemy. However, only one of these is truly functioning at full capacity today: the Strong Tower, the invincible, eternal Tower (God). The slight tower is growing weak and crumbling, no longer offering the saints a refuge where they may enjoy thoughts that mirror God's thoughts and ways that are the ways of God. If a church adopts the ways of the same world it is supposed to oppose, the saints can no longer receive the relief they used to in their church.

In the preceding chapters, we have established the fact that the third generation no longer senses what the first generation did because the latter does not pray as much. Instead, they cut themselves off from God. (That's what not praying does). Consequently, they lose a knowledge of the holy. Yet, at the same time a few sense a need to return to the old ways. They want to know and experience their God, not just promote a moral way of living. What unavoidably ensues is a split.

At the time of this writing, the great Pentecostal movement is at a crossroads. There are two diametrically opposed factions developing: one is liberal and the other conservative. Unless we see a sweeping revival, we will follow the same path that other churches have in their third generation: the church will be fractured.

This pattern can be readily observed in the Bible. Our earlier example of the patriarchs holds true here: Abraham (first generation) and Isaac (second generation) passed on, and then there was a split with Jacob and Esau (third generation).

Later, the monarchy of Israel demonstrated this same cycle. After the reigns of David (first generation) and Solomon (second generation), Rehoboam and Jeroboam (third generation) split the nation.

A Tower Divided Against Itself

The most basic cause of all these splits is a lack of unity. In church splits, the third generation saints lose their unity when they begin to develop vastly different convictions. This potpourri of convictions surfaces because most of the believers base their convictions on elements they do not share in common: their respective pasts and feelings. Everyone has a different past. If everyone bases his convictions on his past, his convictions will, therefore, be as distinct as his past. The same is true of feelings, which are both unique and fickle.

What, then, of the first generation? Did they not have the same extreme diversity of opinion in the area of convictions? No, they did not. Much like the early New Testament believers, they were of one mind, sharing common beliefs and convictions. These common convictions became the mortar that held their tower together, without which it would have crumbled. They shared common convictions because they received them from a common source: the Holy Spirit, who is, according to John 16:7-11, supposed to give us our convictions.

These convictions were not formed by sitting alone contemplating one's past and one's own thoughts. These first generation convictions were procured in prayer. Those believers were, by today's standards, "prayer nuts." The standard believer in those days sat alone talking to God, not to himself. He considered God's thoughts more lofty and more substantial than his own, and so he based his convictions upon the thoughts of God, not his own.

Here is where the problem begins. God will always be a refuge for His people. He will always be a strong tower. This means if the church does not also act as a refuge, we will go to God for our protection from the world. However, we will only live that way for a short time. Just as one abandons old, worn-out, useless flashlight batteries, so will the saints of God abandon a church which offers no refuge and whose pastor has no communication with God. This should not be; God and His churches should both serve as an oasis.

The Eye of the Prophet

A transformation takes place when you spend time with God. Slowly, you begin to think the way God thinks. Your thoughts become His thoughts. For example, the Bible teaches that God hates evil and that the one who truly fears the Lord will hate evil (Prov. 8:13). Yet today very few Christians hate evil. Most of us can't even grasp the notion of despising and loathing evil as God does. We don't hate evil. We tolerate it. We form an indifference toward it. Sometimes, we even flirt with it. Meanwhile, our Heavenly Father is light years away from us in comparison, as a burning rage within Him seethes against evil. The word "hate" is a very strong verb. It transcends "dislike" by miles and is not even in the same category with "indifference." Hate indicates strong, passionate, sometimes uncontrollable emotion. The believer who spends time with God will understand and know this hatred of evil. The believer who neglects to spend time with his God will never know or even begin to understand it.

A bond strengthens in prayer between God and the believer. As he begins to think and act more like God, issues around him become very black and white. For him, "to live is Christ." Either issues around him are for God, or they are against God. Nothing is truly neutral for him; whoever and whatever is not building, is tearing down. Whatever is not for God is against Him. He sees no middle ground because he evaluates life on God's scale of importance: eternity. On such a scale, many things cease to hold the significance they once appeared to hold.

Isaiah was one such man who had what today would be called "an unbalanced theology." (He was head over heels in love with God. How tragically unbalanced!) In Isaiah 26:8, the prophet said, "Yes, Lord, walking in the way of your laws, we wait for you; your name and your renown are the desire of our hearts." In this verse, Isaiah mentioned that he was following God's law, doing things God's way. Furthermore, he said that he wanted God, he wanted His name to be known, and he wanted God to be remembered. These are the things that consumed his life. He didn't look forward to payday or the new camel with four on the floor. Those things were part of life, but were fairly unimportant. The spice of life, the reason to be, was God.

Continuing in verse 9, he says, "My soul longs for you in the night; in the morning, my spirit longs for you." The intensity of this man's desire seemed to breathe right through the page as I read it. He wanted God, day and night. There was nothing in the world that he wanted more. His spirit was continually longing after God; his spirit was continually seeking Him.

However, gears seem to shift as verse 9 continues, and many people begin to misunderstand the prophet at this point. "When your judgments come upon the earth, the people of the world learn righteousness," he says. Here, Isaiah seems rather callous and cold-hearted, almost as if he doesn't care if calamity comes upon people. It seems that compassion for the sinner was Isaiah's weak spot, but that is usually the case for any believer who has the spirit of a prophet. However, at the same time we see that Isaiah's words are the result of a heart and a mind that mirror God's in respect to sin.

In verse 10, he concludes, "Though grace is shown to the wicked, they do not learn righteousness; even in a land of unrighteousness they go on doing evil and regard not the majesty of the Lord." This may seem pessimistic, but it is a sad fact of reality. For many years, our courts in the United States have sentenced our criminals leniently, sometimes giving them little more than a slap on the wrist and a strict warning not to ever, ever let that sort of behavior repeat itself. However, as the Scriptures teach, without judgment they do not learn. That is why Isaiah cries for judgment of God's people because they don't learn without judgment either. It is not a spirit of gloom and doom that motivated him, but a heart for God. He loved God and wanted others to do the same, and he was hurt that the sinfulness of the world hurt God. He was hurt that the world did not perceive the majesty of his God.

Isn't it interesting how the world learns the majesty of God through judgment? When the great sin of the Pentecostal church was made public through such national news items as PTL or Jimmy Swaggart, the world was not as appalled at the sin which was revealed as they were at the way the church handled the situation. Soon the focus was no longer on the so-called "sin" of Jim Bakker but rather on the "Holy Wars" that emerged from it.

The world was probably far more forgiving of Jimmy Swaggart's problem with sexual immorality than the church ever was; however, they began to focus more on how the church was handling his discipline than anything else. Sin is not big news; who doesn't sin? The news is judgment. That which the world discovers as sinful in the church is not the problem. The problem is how the church handles sinfulness. Once a church stops dealing with sin, it no longer shows the world the majesty of God.

We can safely say that the person spending time with God develops the eye of the prophet. He wants his God glorified. He wants his tower (church, pastor) to remain strong, a refuge from the world. His whole thought is that the Church must call sin, "sin."

Open Season on Christians

There is a wild animal preserve just west of my home. It is a refuge, a place of safety for any animal that enters its boundaries. There the animals can find a haven of rest from mankind. They can relax and find shelter from danger. However, the shelter periodically opens its boundaries to the local hunters. Anyone willing to pay the price can have the privilege of hunting the unsuspecting game. Can you imagine the terror that strikes the animals when they suddenly realize that their refuge can no longer provide protection for them?

Animals are not the ones upon whom "open season" has been declared. Christians come to the church because they are weary of this world in which they are strangers. They do not truly understand or like the ways of this foreign land through which they are passing en route to their final destination. They come to church not to forever hide from the world, but to alleviate some of their homesickness (for their eternal home) and to worship their God. However, it seems that today in too many cases, the spiritual leaders of our tower have declared open season on anyone within the boundaries of its refuge. They have opened the door to Satan and all his cohorts. Subsequently, Satan is tracking down and destroying as many unsuspecting Christians as he can.

Today many churches are forsaking their standards of holiness and imitating the world in every way possible. These churches have been transformed from refuges from the world into facsimiles of the world. Those who still desire a refuge from the world are left in conflict with the church.

For example, I know of parents who oppose Christian rock music on the basis that it is unholy to attempt to recycle the world's ways to worship God. These parents are frequently placed in the unhappy position of opposing their church youth groups. I remember one woman telling me about her ten-year-old daughter begging her for a heavy metal Christian rock tape. She resisted for a while but finally gave in when her daughter used the argument that everybody in the youth group had one.

Many parents are faced with a dilemma. They don't want their children listening to this music; however, they can no longer use the church as their refuge. There was a time when if a parent did not want his child following the ways of the world, he could encourage his child to join the youth group at church. The mother I've just referred to found she could not use the church's standards as a refuge or argument against the world.

Those who want a refuge from the world's system are not finding it in many of today's Pentecostal churches. They will soon have to either conform or leave the church the same way they would leave any worldly institution that offers them no refuge. If they want a refuge for their children, they will be pulling them out of their youth groups instead of putting them in.

As I was growing up, my parents provided me with a slight tower from many of the things other young people were doing. It is unlikely that I'll ever be a dancer. Not only do I have two left feet, but they are both weighted down by forces not yet fully understood by man. At any rate, I was at a disadvantage in junior high school because the "sock hop" was the place to go. Seriously lacking the necessary coordination to successfully participate, I tried to back out of it, but my friends were all pushing me towards it.

I was fortunate for a while. A good way to avoid going to a dance was by not asking a girl to go with me. I could just tell my friends that I didn't have a date. The trouble really began on one dreadful Sadie Hawkins Day when a girl asked me!

What could I do? I was trapped. Well, I was almost trapped. My parents wouldn't allow me to go. That became a refuge for me. I told my would-be date and my friends that my parents wouldn't let me go. I made them sound like the villains. (That was in a bygone era in which young people basically respected their elders, so it was an excuse they all accepted.) It would have been quite devastating for me had my parents pushed me towards the world.

Today we need pastors and parents who will be slight towers. I took a position as a youth pastor in South St. Paul, Minnesota, right after I graduated from Bible college. The pastor there never allowed the boys and girls from the youth group to swim together. Many people thought that was quite outdated and backwards. Yet he held his position. It was a bit archaic, but I would prefer that situation to the one in Florida where not only did the youth group swim together, but the pastor's daughter wore a swim suit that became nearly transparent when it got wet. It is truly unfortunate that we cannot ever seem to reach the happy medium; we go from one extreme to another.

When the Cat's Away

By the time I accepted Christ at age 21, I had already participated in all that the world had to offer me. I had finally been set free. My life was no longer a frustration, seeking and searching for happiness, yet never finding it. I was no longer on the world's treadmill. Then, a year after I was saved, I felt a call to Bible college. In college, I constantly ran into young people who were involving themselves in many of the activities which l had forsaken upon meeting Christ. Whenever I talked to them about these things, they used the old argument about being saved by grace and not by works, adding that I was making a mountain out of a mole hill.

I later realized that many of these young people were away from home for the first time in their lives. For the first time ever, they were deciding what their social lives would consist of; their parents weren't. Often, these young people were doing things they would never have done if their parents were around. It's an incarnation of the old cliché, "When the cat's away, the mice will play."

Spiritually, there is a parallel. I believe that today, many of us are separated from our parent (God) because of prayerlessness and are, consequently, doing many things we wouldn't do if we were in His presence more. As a movement we are practicing the absence of God far more than the presence of God. Too many Pentecostals just flatly refuse to pray. Since they don't pray, they stop caring about glorifying God. That's supposed to be the entire reason for us to live. That passionate desire to glorify God should dictate what we do and what we don't do. Many people argue that they can do a certain thing and yet be saved. This very argument reveals the desire of these people's hearts: to stay saved, not to glorify God. The question should not be, "Can I do this and still be saved?" Rather, we should ask, "Can I do this and still glorify God?"

I'm not talking about legalism. I've discovered that holiness without prayer degenerates into legalism. However, legalism with prayer evolves into holiness. When you pray, you begin to conduct your life with one goal in mind: to glorify God. The only true life of holiness comes as a consequence of prayer. Subsequently the life of prayer will keep the slight tower strong.

Chapter VIII

Coming
to God
in Truth

Truth received and not responded to means spiritual declension and loss of capacity. — T. Austin Sparks

In John 4 we find the account of Jesus and the woman at the well. Jesus has just explained to her that if she would drink from what He could give her, she would never thirst again. The woman responded in verse 15 by saying, "Sir, give me this water so that I won't get thirsty and have to keep coming here to draw water."

He told her, "Go, call your husband and come back."

"I have no husband," she replied.

Jesus said to her, "You are right when you say you have no husband. The fact is, you have had five husbands, and the man you now have is not your husband. What you have just said is quite true."

When Jesus pointed out this woman's sin, she was very quick to admit it. She did not try to whitewash it; she simply said, "I have no husband." She did not try to cover her actions at all. She allowed Jesus to reveal the truth about her.

Fooling God

We fool ourselves all the time by trying to fool God. For some reason we are afraid of the truth. We are not truthful with God. We are not truthful with our mates. We are not truthful with our children. The most pathetic situation of all is that we will not be honest with ourselves.

Going back to the preceding account, we find that Jesus is asked by the woman in verse 20 about the proper way to worship God. Jesus responds to her by saying in verse 21, "Believe me, woman, a time is coming when you will worship the Father neither on this mountain nor in Jerusalem. You Samaritans worship what you do not know; we worship what we do know, for salvation is from the Jews."

Many heathens considered certain places peculiarly holy or fit for the worship of their deities. But Jesus was pointing out that the place was a matter of little importance.

The time was at hand in which the spiritual worship of God was about to be established on the earth, and all the rites and ceremonies of the heathens and the Jews were to be abolished entirely.

Jesus was pointing out that worship was no longer going to focus in on a place but rather on an attitude. He brings this out in verses 23 and 24 in which He states, "But a time is coming and has now come when the true worshipers will worship the Father in spirit and truth, for they are the kind of worshipers the Father seeks. God is spirit and His worshipers must worship in spirit and in truth."

Real worship was going to take place in the heart from that moment on. The issue was no longer the outward actions or rituals. The issue was becoming focused on who we are in Christ. So when the woman dealt with the place of worship, Jesus did also. However, His focus was entirely different. The woman was dealing with the physical aspect of her relationship with God, but

Christ was dealing with the spiritual aspect of that relationship. We are not Pentecostal because we raise our hands. Raising our hands may have very little to do with the true worship of God.

We Pentecostals have made the physical aspects of Pentecostal worship something to be attained. Raising our hands does not make us true worshipers. True worshipers worship God two ways: in spirit and in truth.

Much of the focus of the Pentecostal church has been on the spirit. We worship God in spirit; we dance in the spirit; we give in the offering with a right spirit. We even pray in the spirit; however, praying in the spirit goes far beyond just speaking in tongues. We can speak in tongues and not be "in the spirit" at all. Pentecostal worship is that of getting into the spirit of worship. The physical gyrations we put ourselves through may have very little to do with worship. We must enter into the spirit of worship, and to do that we must come to God in truth.

True worship of God is only being done by those people who are truthful in their relationship with God. How can we worship a God that we are lying to? Here is where the problem of worshiping God in spirit comes in. We will never enter into the true spirit of worship if we are not truthful with God. The woman at the well was in much better shape than many Christians today. When Jesus pointed out her sin, she said in essence, "You are right, I'm living in sin."

I once heard Joy Dawson say, "Pride makes truth difficult, humility accepts it." The proud man will rationalize his sin away. He will have a thousand excuses as to why he is the way he is. The humble man will simply admit to his sin. The humble man can enter into worship because he is not putting up a facade.

Renaming Sin

The world and the Church are diligently working to rename sin. Instead of dealing with the truth of the matter, we rename it. If it can be renamed, then it doesn't have to be dealt with. There are no alcoholics in the Church; there are only social drinkers. Nobody has a problem with lust; all we deal with is sexual indiscretion. Renaming sin is like not going all the way with sin. We have this mentality that if a sin is not fully committed, it will not be considered sin by God.

One of the main arguments we give to justify our sin is that of using moderation. "Let your moderation be known to all men" is quickly quoted. I find it interesting that God would say, "You can sin in moderation." That is not God's direction to His people.

I was approached by a woman after a service where I had preached about the problems with social drinking and casual sex. She was quite determined to convince me that anything done in moderation would be acceptable to God.

I said to her, "Is it all right to get drunk in moderation?"

She said, "No, that is an absolute, the Bible clearly states that we should not get drunk."

I then said, "Can a person commit adultery in moderation?"

She answered with the same thought, "No, that also is an absolute."

I said, "Help me to understand what you are saying; you feel it is all right to do that which leads to an absolute as long as the absolute is not committed. Is that correct?"

She said, "Yes, as long as you use moderation."

I then asked her, "The next time your teenage daughter goes out on a date, would you mind if she did everything that led to getting drunk as long as she didn't get drunk, and did everything that led to fornication as long as she didn't fornicate?" Once her double standards were thrust upon her daughter, she no longer liked the idea of moderation.

Isn't it interesting that today because of the AIDS epidemic, the world is saying that the Sexual Revolution is over while at the same time it (pre-marital sex) is exploding in the Church? The Church has often been guilty of condemning the world for the very things it is pursuing.

For years the Church has been telling the world about the evils of alcohol and drugs. Now that the world is seeing the truth of our statement and is coming up with programs such as the national "Just Say No" campaign as well as the M.A.D.D. (Mothers Against Drunk Driving) organization, we are finding, amongst our leaders especially, that alcohol and drugs are commonplace. We are being dubbed as liars and hypocrites. We chafe under such accusations. No hypocrite likes his hypocrisy exposed. This is a description of a Pharisee! We say, "I thank God I'm not like that man over there." We are afraid of truth.

The woman at the well was asking Jesus, "What is the proper way to come to God?"

Jesus said, "It's not a matter of actions anymore; it's a matter of the heart." Jesus was trying to make the point that God now lives in the heart, and the heart becomes the place of worship. That's why He said, "You worship what you do not know, but we worship what we know." Every man knows his own heart. If his heart is not right with God, if there is no truth, he cannot properly worship God. Without truth we will never enter into the true spirit of worship.

When we are living a lie, we find it very difficult to get into the spirit of the place where we are living.

When I was ten years old a neighbor gave my buddies and me a doghouse. He had a Great Dane that died and he no longer needed his large house. This doghouse was big enough for three of us to get inside of so we decided to make it into a clubhouse. The three of us now had a great clubhouse but didn't know what to do with a club so we decided to smoke cigarettes. After about two days of sending smoke signals up to my mom in the house she called me into our house.

She said to me, "What are you boys doing out in your clubhouse?"

I said, "Nothing."

She said, "I believe you boys are doing something I would not approve of. What is it?"

Again I said, "Nothing, Mom!"

Her voice became more determined and she demanded, "Tell me what you are doing out there!"

I looked at the floor and said, "If you think we are smoking cigarettes, you are wrong!"

My mom didn't even bring the smoking issue up. I did. I had been living a lie. It's interesting how a mom can tell when her ten year old is doing something he shouldn't. Once I dealt with it, I could enter back into the spirit of our home. I could go back to being what a ten year old should be.

Sacrifice vs. Obedience

The person who will not deal with truth ultimately deals with great sacrifice. In 1 Samuel 15 we find the account of the prophet Samuel and King Saul. God had instructed King Saul to go and utterly destroy the Amalekites. However, when King Saul returned, it was discovered that he did not utterly destroy them. In verse 10 we read, "Then the word of the Lord came to Samuel: 'I am grieved that I have made Saul king because he has turned away from me and has not carried out my instructions.' "

The next day the prophet was taking this message to Saul. In verse 13 we read that when Samuel reached him, Saul said, "The Lord bless you! I have carried out the Lord's instruction." But Samuel said, "What then is this bleating of sheep in my ears." Samuel knew that Saul had not fully carried out the Lord's instruction.

It is interesting that Saul was fully convinced that he had completely fulfilled them. He even says in verse 15, "The soldiers brought them from the Amalekites; they spared the best of the sheep and cattle to sacrifice to the Lord your God, BUT WE TOTALLY DESTROYED THE REST:" Samuel then tells Saul how God was grieved that He had made him king, and yet Saul still does not get the message.

Still fully convinced that half-sin is not full sin, he says in verse 20, "But I did obey the Lord, I went on the mission the Lord assigned me. I completely destroyed the Amalekites and brought back Agag their king." There was obviously a lack of understanding between the prophet and king.

Saul said that he brought back these few things so that he could sacrifice them to God. Samuel then makes his now famous statement, "Does the Lord delight in burnt offerings and sacrifices us much as in obeying the voice of the Lord? To obey is better than sacrifice."

It's not that God does not want sacrifice. It's that obedience is better than sacrifice in that, OBEDIENCE GOES BEFORE SIN; SACRIFICE GOES AFTER IT. If Saul had simply obeyed God, it would not have been necessary to make a sacrifice. No matter how we try to justify our sin today, it will be the first thing we sacrifice once God has us on our knees. What we are finding in Christianity today are people who will search the Scriptures to justify their lifestyles and yet not search their hearts to find their God.

Sins of Immorality

Whenever we justify our sin, we will live in a world of sacrifices. Since we don't fully put to death those things which appeal to our flesh, we will constantly be asking God to forgive us for our involvement in them. In Romans 13 we find Paul giving us some godly advice. In verses 13 and 14 he says, "Let us behave decently, as in the daytime, not in orgies and drunkenness, not in sexual immorality and debauchery, not in dissension and jealousy. Rather, clothe yourself with the Lord Jesus Christ, and do not think about how to gratify the desires of the sinful nature."

Instead of clothing ourselves with Jesus Christ, we make provision for the flesh to fulfill the lust of it. People who have a drinking problem often find they pattern their lives so as to make it easy to drink. I know of one pastor who had a man come and talk to him about his drinking problem. The man said, "Pastor, I don't understand what's wrong with me, but every time I go into a bar, I can't help but drink." The lady who can't break her attraction to soap operas finds she has a television in every room of her house. The man with a lust problem often has a satellite dish in his back yard or is tuned-in each night to the dark side of the Internet.

In Galatians 6:17 we find a struggle we are all faced with, "For the sinful nature desires what is contrary to the Spirit, and the Spirit what is contrary to the sinful nature. They are in conflict with each other, so that you do not do what you want." We have this constant struggle going on inside us. Our flesh does not want to seek God. Our Spirit does. The one we give into, whether the flesh or the spirit, will determine what comes out of our lives.

Two verses later we read of what our lives will produce if we give into the desires of the flesh more than the spirit. "The acts of the sinful nature are obvious: sexual immorality, impurity and debauchery." These are the very things Paul tells us in Romans that we will have to turn away from. In a prayerless church, a church that gives itself more to the desires of the flesh than the spirit, sexual immorality is quite common.

I find it interesting that King Saul was instructed to utterly destroy the Amalekites. The Amalekites were very immoral people. They represent the constant struggle man has with his flesh. The Amalekites were always fighting against God's people. Saul would not utterly destroy them; thus, we still struggle today with our sexuality. Today we keep hard-core pornography out of our Christian homes, but as a family we sit down together and watch "Married With Children." We still make provisions for the flesh, and subsequently we will constantly struggle with the grip the flesh has on us. Until we obey, we will live in a world of sacrifices.

The Sacrifice God Accepts

King David lived in a world of sacrifices. David had his problems with obeying God. However, David had a heart for God and eventually learned what God was looking for.

In Psalm 51:17 we read, "The sacrifices of God are a broken spirit [the true worshipers come to God in spirit]; a broken and contrite heart, [they come to God in truth], O God, you will not despise."

David was honest with God. We will never shock God with truth. If we decide to tell God about our problem with sin, we will not set God back on His throne in astonishment. God is not about to say, "I didn't know that about you." We must come to God in truth, otherwise, we will not let God deal with us. If I am trying to hide my sin from God, then I will refuse any help from Him because to accept His help is to admit to my sin.

We must ask ourselves, "Do we want to be one of the true worshipers of God?" If we do, then we must go to Him with our hearts open. We must allow God to minister to us. God never reveals sin to bring judgment upon us. God reveals sin for one purpose: to bring repentance and reconciliation. God does not want to condemn us to hell anymore than we would want to send our own children to damnation.

Chapter IX

Your Concept of God

> *There was no fire, no light in the room; nevertheless, it appeared to me as if it were perfectly light . . . it seemed as if I met the Lord Jesus Christ face to face.*
> — Charles Finney, in prayer

What is your concept of God? What do you believe about God? You may wish to consider these questions carefully before you read this chapter because they form the heart of it. Your concept of God will determine your faith in God and your worship of Him. That makes your concept very important and an understanding of where it comes from even more important.

Where Concept Comes From

In his book, *What Ever Happened to Worship?* A.W. Tozer develops an interesting thought by saying, "No church can rise above its religion." Most people receive their concept of God from their church or denomination. A person is generally able to have faith in God only to the degree that his church does. Generally a person who attends a Baptist or Lutheran Church will not believe in divine healing or speaking in tongues. Why? Simply because that person's church does not teach it. On the other hand, a person who attends a Four Square, Assembly of God, or any other Pentecostal church will believe most fervently in such divine manifestations. Why? Again, because his church teaches it.

Your faith in God is limited to your concept of God. No church can rise above its own level of faith. If your pastor preaches that divine healing is a manifestation of God limited to the days of the Apostles, then it is likely that you will believe this also. This will mold your concept of God. You believe God is omnipotent, but for some reason He just doesn't heal people anymore. As a result, you will not have the faith that would lead you to pray for healing.

If you grew up in the church, then the church became your main source in developing your concept. However, if you were saved at a later date in life, you find that the person who led you to Christ became your first source. This was true for me. Everything I believed hinged on what Bill Ellerman, my spiritual father, believed. If Bill didn't believe something was so, it just plain wasn't so! I became very dependent upon Bill, unable to stand alone. I could see only as much of God as he saw.

Elijah and Elisha

As they were walking along together, suddenly a chariot of fire and horses of fire appeared and separated the two of them, and Elijah went up to heaven in a whirlwind. Elisha saw this and cried out, "My Father! My Father! The chariots and horsemen of Israel!" And Elisha saw him no more. Then, he took hold of his own clothes and tore them apart. He took the cloak that had fallen from Elijah and went back and stood on the bank of the Jordan. Then he took the cloak that had fallen from him and struck the water with it. "Where is the Lord, the God of Elijah?" he asked. When he struck the water, it divided to the right and to the left, and he crossed over (2 Kings 2:11-14).

Elisha had just witnessed the power of God. God had displayed His strength in parting the waters, in taking Elijah up in the chariot of fire, and yet Elisha called out for the God of Elijah. Why didn't he cry, "Where is the Lord, my God?" It is because Elisha was dependent on Elijah for his concept of God even as I was dependent on Bill. Hence, we see that even as far back as 500 B.C. (the time of Elisha), God's people have relied on one another for their concept of God.

This is not bad in and of itself. We all begin this way but God expects us to reach a point at which we develop our own revelation or concept of Him. Unfortunately, most Christians today only see as much of God as their spiritual parent, their pastor, or their favorite television evangelist.

Hearsay vs. Revelation

What I just described is a hearsay concept of God. It is a notion about God that is built upon what a third party (i.e., not you or God, the first and second parties) has to say about God. I'm not saying that such concepts of God contradict God's true nature or character. They may or may not. However, that's not the real problem. The real problem with a hearsay concept is that it's like seeing a Xerox copy of a Da Vinci painting instead of the original masterpiece. Although the Xerox copy probably won't distort the painting beyond recognition, it just won't do it justice. There will be things in the original that won't be seen on that black and white copy. The copy, at best, will give the casual observer a basic idea about what the painting is.

As I said, my concept of God was mostly a theological assent to what my spiritual parent believed. But then, God placed in me a craving to know Him for myself. I knew a lot about God from what I heard my spiritual elders say, but I didn't know Him. Similarly, you might say I know a lot about the president of our country from what I've heard about him on the news, but I don't know the president. I was tired of knowing about God. I wanted a direct revelation of God from God — not from another Christian. I was consumed with this craving to know Him for myself.

I don't believe it is possible to build a relationship with anyone (especially God) if you don't converse with that individual. When we want to build a relationship with a person, we talk, we do things together, and usually find that as we spend more time with that person, we become more like him or her.

This wonderful communication we treat so mundanely is our opportunity to interact with God. It's also His opportunity to interact with us. In writing a book so heavily built upon prayer, I realize that I have the potential to play down the importance of God's Word. There's nothing I want to do less. However, without a proper balance of both the Word and prayer, we will develop a wrong concept of God.

Inaccurate Concept of God

For the past two decades the focus of the Church has been on the Word of God to the exclusion of prayer. This has resulted in a very human concept of God. The Word of God deals with the fleshly aspect of God. The Word became flesh. Because of a focus on God's Word only, we have developed a very fleshly approach to God. This is why there are whole movements that deal strictly with what God wants to do to satisfy our flesh.

Think of all the theology developed lately that focuses on the flesh. We have become far more concerned with comfort than with character. The Word of God gives us the human concept of God. Prayer reminds us of the deity of God. Today, because of the lack of prayer, we have lost sight of the deity of Christ. From the lack of prayer and the Word, we have developed a concept of God that is off-center. This off-centered concept has allowed certain "ministries" to arise such as Christian rock music. Ministries that have a wrong concept of God then develop wrong concepts of God in the lives of those they bring to Christ. Mistakes like these are very serious because our concept of God determines how we worship God.

If we are not seeing God as He is and developing a concept of Him that is true to His nature, then we will see Him as He is not. The result will be that we will offer Him offensive worship (strange fire) that clashes with His true nature. That is just what happened 3,000 years ago when the children of Israel were wandering through the desert.

> Aaron's sons Nadab and Abihu took their censers, put fire in them and added incense; and they offered unauthorized fire before the Lord, contrary to his command. So fire came out from the presence of the Lord and consumed them, and they died before the Lord. Moses then said to Aaron, "This is what the Lord spoke when he said, 'Among those who approach me, I will show myself holy; in the sight of all the people I will be honored' " (Lev. 10:1-3).

Notice Moses' response to Aaron when he says, "This is what the Lord spoke when he said, 'Among those who approach me, I will show myself holy.' " In essence, Moses is telling Aaron not to be surprised at what happened to his boys because God has said that anybody who worships Him must treat Him as holy. Aaron's sons came before God offering Him strange fire or worship that is not in character with who God really is. God will not accept worship that is contrary to His true nature.

Entire ministries (such as Christian rock music) are rising and propagating concepts of God that have been dictated by people's feelings about God. These ministries are not spreading a concept of God that they have received from God, but rather are distributing a concept of God which reinforces their own interests and lifestyles. People who are brought to the Lord by these ministries end up with the same concept of God as the one espoused by these ministries. It is not a matter of whether or not they are bringing people to Christ. It is a matter of what kind of concept of God they are developing in these young minds. Today we have a rock-and-roll God.

Converts won through rock music will defend that music. Many have asked me why they defend it. I believe there are two reasons:

(1) People generally regard anything that brought them to the Lord as being sacred.

(2) Christianity, as they know it, must somehow by definition include Christian rock music. As long as they've been Christians, rock music has been part of the normal scene. In a way, it is part of their heritage, so they will defend it just the same as any person will defend his religion.

Worship Through Revelation

Consider the experience of Isaiah recorded in Isaiah 6. He had a supernatural revelation of God in which the Lord was surrounded by seraphim crying, "Holy, holy, holy is the Lord almighty." That was what he wrote down — what was revealed to him.

Church history teaches us that whenever God revealed himself afresh, it changed our worship of Him. The distinctive characteristic of this worship was its music. A great number of our classic hymns are the work of Charles Wesley. He did not write them to make a quick buck, nor did he write them to find favor with the world. Instead, he wrote them as the Church was revived by a new revelation of God. God revealed himself in a new way to what was becoming an increasingly stale Church. (We usually refer to this as "revival.") This new, exciting revelation of God changes our concept of God. This is what motivated Charles Wesley to write songs. His brother Jonathan was bringing the revival in with his preaching; Charles was writing songs of worship that boldly declared praises to the special attributes of God which he revealed. Those hymns were a result of a concept of God that was based on revelation knowledge.

We can see this same thing in the worship of Martin Luther.

He wrote "A Mighty Fortress is Our God" as a result of a revelation of God. On the night before he was to appear before an inquisition of the Roman Catholic Church, he spent much time fearfully praying to God, and, in response, God revealed himself as a "mighty fortress." Most of our worship today is, sadly enough, a result of "feelings" about God with no real heaven-sent revelation or even biblical truth for support.

What Should We Do?

God wants us to have our own revelation of Him, not some warmed-over revelation that was somebody else's. But make no mistake about it — the only way we'll ever have our own revelation of God is through prayer and the Word. There's no short cut. If we are not pray-ers, we need to consider carefully our ministry to others. If we don't see God as He is, how can we show others who God really is?

We may be leading them into false worship. Our worship is an expression of our concept of God. Do you believe God is a "toe-tapping, get down, get with it," type of God? Or do you see Him as Isaiah did, high and lifted up, with His train filling the temple as angels sang out, "Holy, holy, holy is our God"?

What should we do? We should do the same thing the men of God did to get their revelation. When Moses met God, he spent 40 years in the desert getting to know God. Then and then only did he become the greatest leader the ancient Israelis ever had. He was able to lead others because God was able to lead him.

What about Paul? When he met Jesus, he went out into the desert where he spent three years getting to know God. After that — not before — he emerged as the most prolific writer of the New Testament. He could show others God because he let God show himself to him.

We must go to the desert of prayer and get alone with our God. We must allow God to reveal himself to us. We must develop a right concept of Him. There is no other way than by spending intimate time with Him. We have no choice. We must become people of prayer.

Chapter X

God
Working
in Us

For it is God which worketh in us both to will and to do of his good pleasure. — Paul the Apostle, A.D. 61

As a young preacher right out of Bible college, I had the same types of thoughts toward my own ministry as did other young preachers. We wanted to change the world. We all wanted to take Billy Graham's place.

For many years I prayed that God would use me. As a Pentecostal preacher I also prayed for the gifts of the Spirit to be manifest in my ministry. My whole thought was that if I were going to attract big crowds, I would need these gifts. I would say, "God, I want the Word of knowledge; I want a Word of wisdom; give me the gift of healing." I would pray that quite often.

The thing that would really frustrate me the most is that the more I prayed for the gifts, the more God would say, "Seek Jesus."

"But God, I need the gifts to be an effective minister," I would respond.

God kept saying over and over, "Seek Jesus; seek my Son."

I never understood the difference between seeking Jesus and seeking the gifts. As it turned out, I wanted God to work through me while God wanted to work in me. Wanting God to simply work through us is a pursuit of our own comfort. Wanting God to work in us is a pursuit of character development.

In this self-serving society we strive for comfort far more than character. The thought of depriving ourselves for the purpose of seeking God is foreign to us. We would much rather be served than serve. Subsequently, the pursuit of gifts becomes most natural. We don't have to earn gifts. We don't even have to deserve them. The whole thought of being used by God is very appealing to the flesh. However, God can use anybody. God can work through a donkey. God working through us is not the problem; God working in us is.

To be totally honest with you, I pursued the gifts to make others think I was spiritual. When I was an associate pastor in Minnesota, I would watch evangelists come through our church who were being used by God. This was during the heart of the Charismatic move, and the gifts of the Spirit were flowing quite readily. I began to desire this for my own ministry. I found myself wanting others to think I was spiritual more than really wanting to do something for God.

This is not an unusual thought. Consider a man named Simon in the book of Acts.

> When Simon saw this, that the Holy Spirit was given when the apostles placed their hands upon people's heads, he offered money to buy this power. "Let me have this power too," he exclaimed, "so that when I lay my hands on people, they will receive the Holy Spirit." But Peter replied, "May your money perish with you for thinking God's gift can be bought!" (Acts 8:18 20).

The pursuit of the gifts can possibly be for our own comfort. If I can convince you that I am spiritual, I can also convince you to send me all your money. You say, "But a true man of God would never do that." I believe you are right. A true man of God would never misuse the gifts. A true man of God would make character development his primary goal.

True spirituality cannot be bought. However, the gifts of the Spirit are a natural part of our experience. A problem occurs when the gift becomes our goal rather than the giver. We tend to focus more on God using us than on God himself. We become far more concerned with a Word of knowledge than with love, joy, and peace.

Consider what I Corinthians 13 teaches us. In verse 1 we read, "Though I speak with the tongues of men and of angels, and have not charity, I am become as sounding brass, or a tinkling cymbal." The emphasis here is on character rather than the gifts. In verse 2 the same thought is carried on: "And though I have the gift of prophecy, and understand all mysteries, and all knowledge; and though I have all faith, so that I could remove mountains, and have not charity, I am nothing:"

First Corinthians 13 is called the "Love Chapter" because its whole emphasis is on the fact that the gifts of the Spirit are of no value without the character (love) of Christ. Even if the gifts are in operation, the thing that impresses God is not what He can do through us but rather what He can do in us.

First Corinthians 13:11 says, "When I was a child, I spake as a child, I understood as a child, I thought as a child; but when I became a man, I put away childish things." I remember once when my son was only four years old. It was just one week after Christmas when Ronnie was talking to his mom. "Mommy, let's talk," Ronnie said.

"What should we talk about?" asked his mom.

He looked at her with a longing in his eyes and said, "Let's talk about what I'm going to get next year for Christmas."

As a child we speak as children. My own immaturity in Christ caused me to talk as a child. "God, give me gifts." "God, let's talk all about what You want to give me."

Empires Through Giftedness

Gifts can build empires. Look at the gifted men who have built huge ministries upon their own giftedness. This is where Paul's statement, "You can have the faith that moves mountains but if you do not have love, [if you have not developed in the character of Christ] it is nothing" becomes quite important.

Nothing will last that is not built upon the character of Christ. Consider the ministries that have fallen from the lack of one of the characteristics of God — self-control. The leader of one of these ministries turned in the leader of another ministry because of sin in his life. To further prove that many of these ministries lack God's character, they are now taking each other to court. They are upset with each other because they took each other's gift away. It's like two children fighting over their toys.

If they had concerned themselves with developing God's character, there would be no need for vengeance. Nobody can take away your character. When a ministry is built upon the character of God, it will go on without you.

I remember Rev. Owen Carr telling us in Bible college about pastoring the Stone Church in Chicago. He had labored for many years with hardly any success. Finally, God began to pour out His spirit on that church. It was what he had worked and prayed for, for many years. In the midst of the revival, God called him to a different work. Owen began to argue with God, saying, "God, I can't leave now; we are in the midst of revival." God said, "Why can't you leave in the midst of revival?" Owen said, "Because it will die if I leave now." God said, "If this revival is going because of you, it needs to die anyway."

Owen realized that ministry must be built upon God working in us instead of just through us. Owen went from that church to start a Christian-based television ministry in Chicago. Both ministries are still doing great things for God — without Owen Carr.

It is very common to hear people refer to ministries, saying things like, "They could never exist without the person who started them." That may be true if mere man is the force behind them.

However, no man can take away your ministry when it is built upon the character of Christ in you. But through the lack of character, you can lose your whole livelihood.

The Key to Effectiveness

The key is not what God does through us. The key is what God does in us. When a person spends great amounts of time in prayer, it changes his ministry. He becomes far more effective because through spending time in the presence of God people tend to see Jesus in us. It's not that fasting or prayer makes a person a better speaker; it's that prayer and fasting denote self-denial. Thus, character is developed.

Because we focus so much on the gifts, we have equated them with spirituality. In other words, if you are spiritual, you will be used in the gifts. Due to the lack of prayer, many Pentecostal preachers are afraid of stepping out in faith for fear God will not work through them with the gifts, thus causing them to seem unspiritual. I have talked with many pastors who rarely pray for their people to be baptized in the Holy Spirit for fear they won't receive it. The problem we face is that we need the gifts. They help us in the ministry. I believe in the gifts of the spirit. I am Pentecostal. It's just that the gifts are meant to be a result of going after God. People need to see Jesus in us.

What God Sees or Man Sees

When we focus on God working through us, we primarily concern ourselves with what man sees. When we focus on God working in us, we primarily concern ourselves with what God sees. If all I concern myself with is what man sees, then all I have to do is guard my steps — and not get caught.

In my first book *Prayer Can Change Your Marriage*, I publicly admitted that as a minister I was sneaking off to see "R" rated movies and having problems with the flesh. Do you know why I used to do those things? Because I was quite sure l could do it without getting caught. That was when I concerned myself with what men saw.

Then 1 began to seek God. I began to pray, and suddenly I found myself under great conviction. So much so that I chose to confess my weakness to my wife all on my own. I even published it in my book. God has used my confession to minister to countless men and women, because when God prompts us to repentance, all men accept it. However, when man forces us to repentance, nobody believes it.

This is why we have such a hard time believing that ministers who get caught in sin really repent. The question will always remain, "Would they have stopped if nobody had found out?"

A Person of Prayer

If I want God to work in me, I must be a man of prayer. Proverbs 16:6 teaches us that "Through the fear of the Lord, a man avoids evil." Prayer is the active practice of fearing God. To fear God is to pray. It develops great reverence for God; it develops great respect for God. Suddenly we find that we conduct ourselves according to what God sees, not according to what man sees.

When we live in the fear of the Lord, we turn from iniquity. When we live in the fear of man, we have to get caught before we will quit. Our love of man (even our own family) will never keep us from sin. We must develop a deep love for God.

> Different kinds of fruit trees can quickly be identified by examining their fruit. A variety that produces delicious fruit never produces an inedible kind. And a tree producing an inedible kind can't produce what is good. So the trees having the inedible fruit are chopped down and thrown on the fire. Yes, the way to identify a tree or a person is by the kind of fruit produced (Matt. 7:17-20).

The kind of fruit we produce is determined by how much time we spend in the presence of God. God must always be our objective. Never the gifts. We must let the gifts flow out of a right relationship with God.

Chapter XI

Diligently Seeking God

Our praying needs to be pressed and pursued with an energy that never tires, a persistency which will not be denied, and a courage which never fails. — E.M. Bounds

When I was a boy, one of my favorite stories was "Aladdin and the Magic Lamp" from *Tales of the Arabian Nights*. On a rainy day I could read it time after time and still get the same thrill out of it. I think we all know the story about the boy who found the magic lamp in which a genie resided. The genie, of course, granted Aladdin three wishes, and the rest is history. What baffled me was the lack of any real relationship between Aladdin and the genie. I thought it would be neat to have a genie as a friend. Yet Aladdin and the genie never socialized and never really developed a friendship. Their only communication was initiated by Aladdin when he was in a tight spot and needed something. He was interested only in getting as much as he could out of the genie. It appeared sort of selfish and insensitive to me even as a boy.

Yet many of us Christians are guilty of the same selfishness and insensitivity. Tragically, we treat our God and Father like a genie in a magic lamp. Like young Aladdin with his genie in the little story, we often have no "social" relationship with our God. We call on Him only when we're in a tight spot and need something.

So many of us are seeking things from God under the pretense of seeking God. When we are sick, we seek healing from God. When hard financial times hit, we seek money from God. We call this seeking God, but this is really light years from truly seeking God. The one who truly seeks God expects only one thing: God. He is looking for God, not just the things God can give him. The prayer of the seeker's life is, "God, I just want You." When was the last time you prayed that prayer? I believe God wants to reveal himself to us, but most of us just aren't interested.

It has always been my contention that we share a common trait with God in relationships. Any time we begin a new relationship we are hesitant to reveal very much about who we really are. However, if that relationship begins to develop and we recognize that this person is truly interested in who we are, we begin to tell this person things about ourselves that we would tell no one else. In the same way, God is hesitant to reveal very much of himself to any casual seeker who can "take Him or leave Him." However, when a person is truly interested in seeing who He is, he will seek Him in prayer. To such a person, God will reveal himself in dynamic ways.

Crisis Pray-ers

One of the greatest weaknesses of Christians today is caused by our undue concern with the affairs of this world. Frequently, our jobs demand so much from us that there is no time left for God. Other times, our social lives, that football game or TV show we can't miss, or our hobbies, devour our time. We fold our arms, raise our eyebrows, and sigh, "It's not my fault I'm not praying.

There just aren't enough hours in the day." But when one of our children is seriously ill, or we receive a salary cut at work, or we are diagnosed as terminally ill, the day seems to expand. Suddenly, there's time enough to pray. When things get bad enough, we pray. We are then what I call "crisis pray-ers," a people with sporadic prayer lives, bouncing from crisis to crisis.

If we only pray when we are in the midst of crisis, we develop the idea that prayer is just an "SOS" to God. Consequently, we never pray unless there is a disaster so great that we need to transmit a distress call to God. We're left with the misconception that prayer is a communication used exclusively as a remedy for overwhelming tragedy.

Not only does this limit the amount of time we pray, but it hurts the quality of our prayers as well. During tragedy we focus our prayers on the urgent and tend to ignore the important. It may be urgent that we receive a sum of money or that someone we know receives a healing, but it is also very important to just sit back and tell God how much we love and need Him. During a crisis, praying an "important" rather than an "urgent" prayer is difficult. That's why we need to develop a prayer life in non-crisis times. There's nothing wrong with praying during a crisis (in fact, we must!), but if that's the only time we pray, there's something wrong.

Crisis-Produced Prayer Meetings

One day, my dad, who worked with my mom at a Bible college, telephoned me to tell me about a tremendous financial problem they had which threatened the school. The need was so urgent that a special series of faculty-student prayer meetings was called. As my dad was telling me about this, the Holy Spirit impressed me with a thought: *What will happen to these prayer meetings as soon as God honors their prayers by meeting their need?*

The same thing seems to happen all the time. We call prayer meetings when we're in a jam. God meets our need. We call off the prayer meetings because we're no longer in a jam. This demonstrates a point that seems quite ironic to me. Our primary goal is to see that we resolve our conflict, and we use prayer as a means to achieve this goal. God's goal, on the other hand, is to see us pray, and He takes advantage of our conflicts to achieve that goal. Our big concern is getting our needs met, while God's concern is to get us to spend time with Him. He is most concerned about our prayer lives.

These transitory crisis prayer meetings are a reflection of ailing individual prayer lives. If prayer is not a regular part of our lives, we often feel the need for special prayer meetings. If prayer is a regular part of our lives, when a special need arises it will simply slide into our ongoing prayers. Such a lifestyle of prayer will stand fast because it is based on a commitment to a life of prayer. But these special prayer meetings will always be transitory because they are based on commitment to a crisis. When the crisis ends, the prayer meetings will always end with it.

There is another reason why crisis pray-ers quit praying as soon as their crisis passes: they are just plain exhausted. Crisis praying is very hard on a person simply because of the tremendous tension and stress the crisis has caused. But when we only pray during a crisis, we assume that prayer is always that exhausting. Most think, *Why, prayer is simply too hard to engage in every day!* However, that notion can't be right because Jesus said, "My burden is light" (Matt. 11:30). The only way to exchange our heavy burden for His light one is to make prayer a daily practice.

Crisis pray-er, consider what would happen in your life if after the next crisis you continued to pray in the same way you did during the crisis. I believe you could experience the abundant life Jesus came to bring you. You would not only see God answer your prayer by removing and resolving your crisis, but every day you would be investing precious time in His presence which would work to keep you from the next crisis!

A Lifestyle of Seeking God

Dick Eastman's "Change the World School of Prayer" challenged me to develop a regular prayer life. Dick spent two days at our church teaching this seminar on the importance of prayer. By the conclusion of that second day, I was determined to invest my life in really seeking God.

After about two months of spending one or two hours praying each day, I found myself boasting to God about how well I was doing. I remember beaming, "God, I'm diligently seeking You now." God pulled the proverbial rug out from under my feet, though, by speaking to my heart. "Ron," He said, "you've hardly scratched the surface of what it takes to diligently seek Me." God had to bring me to the place where I was praying at least one hour a day before I could even hear God say, "Ron, you're just beginning." Before He brought me to that place, I was so far out of touch with Him that I could never have heard Him.

Diligently seeking God is more than what we do during our prayer time. Seeking God becomes a lifestyle. It becomes a mindset that permeates all activities of life. It grows into a passionate, all-consuming trek, searching after the One in whose hands the fate of the universe lies. It is this drive that leads us to make (not find) time for God. One who is seeking God doesn't do it in his spare time, when there's nothing else to do.

Oak Trees Don't Grow Overnight

We live in an age of instant pudding, instant milk, instant cereal, and a host of other "instant" food products. To speed up the heating of the instant food that requires cooking, we even have microwave ovens. Then because we don't have very much time between the moment we put our food in the oven and take it out, we have remote control devices that allow us to operate our living room TV sets from the kitchen. We are an instant people living in an instant world, and this sometimes affects our faith.

Often we go to the altar to pray, but if God can't compete with our microwave's most recent speed record, we give up and seek to answer the prayer ourselves, proclaiming it a step of faith. But sometimes it simply takes time, and we have to be willing to take a real step of faith: trusting God and waiting for Him to answer.

This is also true when we're seeking God not just for things, but just for who He is. It takes time. There's no quick, easy short-cut. If it didn't take time, seeking God could hardly be described as a "diligent" effort.

Don Meyer was forever fond of saying, "Oak trees don't grow overnight, but weeds do." The more I grow in the Lord, the more I see the truth of that statement.

What God Doesn't Know CAN Hurt Us

Worship is a tremendously important part of seeking God. The Lord inhabits the praises of His people, so it's fair to say that worship generates the presence of God. That's one reason why those who want God have a tendency to worship God more than those who don't. These people want to be in His presence, where they can get to know Him. If a believer fails to worship regularly, he develops a very cold heart and drifts very far from His God. This is also true of churches that tend to downplay worship collectively. Those churches tend to become very stale and very distant from God. We who wish to seek God must lift our hands, hearts, and voices in united praise and adoration to our God.

> Yet a time is coming and has now come when the true worshipers will worship the Father in Spirit and truth, for they are the kind of worshipers the Father seeks. God is spirit, and his worshipers must worship in spirit and truth (John 4:23-24).

Jesus said that God is seeking worshipers. That means He's not just indifferent about it. He's not just sitting around nonchalantly waiting for worshipers. He's seeking them! That, in and of itself, constitutes a call to worship as far as we are concerned. Moreover, God is not seeking just any kind of worshipers. He is seeking true worshipers, those who will worship Him in spirit and in truth. If we are going to seek God, we must worship Him. If we are going to worship Him, we must worship Him in spirit and in truth. Yet in the Church today, our worship is particularly weak in that last category: truth.

In Psalm 51:3, David acknowledges his sin, saying, "My sin is ever before me." Like David, we feel that our sin stands out like a sore thumb. Whenever we go to prayer, the first thing that comes to mind is what rotten villains we are in comparison to Jesus and how we have fallen short of the glory of God. We are often bitter or afraid to trust God yet won't admit it to Him. We worship under false pretense, assuming that what God doesn't know can't hurt us.

Did you know that we can never surprise God? Some Christians have the idea that if they were to be really candid with the Lord about who and what they are, He would be shocked! Suppose one day you get real honest with God and say, "Lord, there is something I haven't told you, but I have a terrible temper. I just can't imagine God standing in heaven with His mouth hanging open and His hands set firmly on His hips saying, "I didn't know that about you!" He already knows all about us. We can't surprise Him or fool Him.

Therefore, God won't think less of us if we talk to Him about our bad temper, our fear, our jealousy, or our bitterness. He already knows all about it and is waiting for us to come to Him with the problem. When we go to God in truth, then God can work in our lives. I'm not saying that He is unable to work in our lives if we don't go to Him in truth. He always has the ability to work in any "hidden" area of our lives. The real problem is that when we are trying to hide something from Him we won't accept the help He is able to provide. In order to accept His help, we must admit we have a problem.

"Search Me, O God"

If we truly want God, we must open our hearts to God and give Him free reign in every aspect of our lives. There can be no areas of our lives that we're "not going to bother God with."

Search me, O God, and know my heart; test me
and know my anxious thoughts (Ps. 139:23).

That verse is a daily part of my life. It's not something I pray once and for all. I must daily pray and open my heart to my Father. Unfortunately, most Christians don't do this. They won't open all of their hearts. Instead, they present God with a *"Reader's Digest"* version. They open selected portions of their hearts and no more. Some refuse to ask God to search their hearts and check their motives. Others refuse to open their hearts and bring their own problems to God in prayer, but they bring the problems of others to Him.

I have met self-proclaimed prayer warriors who claim to spend many hours in prayer daily, and yet their lives are packed with all types of problems: family problems, church problems, personal problems, and the list goes on and on. These are the results of an unbalanced prayer life.

Anybody can spend time with God (even if they have to force themselves to do it!) but those who are really developing their relationship with God are those who are asking God to look into their own hearts. These people aren't spending all their time asking God to take care of other people's problems. They are letting God take care of their problems as well. They are an open book to the Lord. They're allowing God to search *their* hearts from ceiling to cellar.

As God searches our hearts, He brings to our attention hindrances in our relationship with Him. It is absolutely crucial that these hindrances be eliminated, or else we will never have a ministry of intercessory prayer which is operating at maximum efficiency. The more we allow God to thusly transform us into the image of His Son, the more powerful our prayers will become.

"Test Me"

The second part of Psalm 139:23 says, "Test me and know my anxious thoughts." The phrase "anxious thoughts" can be translated "desires" in this text. It is important to realize that desire is more than a simple wish. It is a deep-seated craving, an intense longing. This sheds new light on this verse. The Psalmist is essentially saying, "God, look into my heart and know the things that are deep-seated longings. Put me to the test on these desires. I will pay any price to have these desires fulfilled."

When we desperately want something with all of our being, we're ready to pay any price to get it. Desire is what leads us to pay whatever price is required to obtain something. That was the position of the Psalmist. He was consumed with a longing, but not for a house or something material. He was obsessed with a longing for God, and he was telling God he'd pay whatever price was required to satisfy that longing.

In his book *The Necessity of Prayer*, E.M. Bounds writes that desire goes before prayer. Desire gradually builds until it breaks forth into prayer. Desire is silent — prayer is the verbal expression of the desire of our heart. Our failure to pray stems from our lack of desire for God. We've reached a sort of passive indifference on which we profess our love for God, but deep down in our hearts we have no burning desire for Him.

Yet despite the absence of this desire, the constituency of our movement is involved in prayer. If such desire is a prerequisite to prayer and we do not have that desire, what, then, prompts us to prayer? Things! As I mentioned earlier. we seek things from God, usually when we're in a crisis. But prayer prompted by things is transitory at best. We quit praying when we get the thing we want. On the other hand, prayer that is prompted by a great longing for God leads us into regular, continual prayer.

Why do you think we have developed so much theology on faith today? We believe that if we properly exercise faith, we can obtain the thing we want without having to spend much time at it. Subsequently, we are saying today that if we pray more than once about something, it is a lack of faith. This theology is birthed out of a thing-seeking society. Such theology effectively prevents us from really knowing our God. Under that theology we could only pray, "God, I want to know You," once.

Supposedly, to pray that prayer more than once would indicate a lack of faith. But the fact is, we must spend time seeking God to know Him. What we are talking about is relationship, not mechanics. Knowing God takes more than one little "faith" prayer.

"Lord, How Long?"

It's not uncommon to ask the question, "How long, Lord, am I going to have to pray and seek you?"

Bill Gothard once shared a story from his childhood that answered this question. Bill and his brother shared a room while they were growing up. Whereas Bill was very neat, his brother was very messy. Half the room looked like a museum, and the other half looked like the site of a Civil War battle. This bothered Bill, so he decided to make his brother's bed every morning to show him how much he loved him (also hoping his brother would start making his own bed). After doing this for several weeks with no response from his brother, Bill was a bit discouraged and went to talk to God about it. He asked the Lord how long he would have to make his brother's bed. God answered him with a question: "Why are you making his bed?" Bill replied, "Because I want to show him I love him." God, in turn, said, "How long do you intend to love him?"

How long are you going to pray and seek God? You can answer this question by determining how long you intend to love Him. The degree to which you love and want God will determine the time you spend in prayer.

It's time to stop seeking things and start seeking God. It's time to start seeking the healer instead of the healing. It's time to stop seeking the gifts and, instead, seek the giver. Once you have God, you have all that He possesses.

Part Two

Chapter XII

The Solution

I have had the privilege of teaching prayer seminars literally throughout the world. I have preached in small churches and large churches, in rural and in urban areas. Yet, in all my travels I have noticed one particular constant: the attitude of pastors toward prayer. No matter what region of the country I'm in, I hear pastors say, "I just don't pray as much as I should." This tells me the greatest problem the Church is facing: prayerless pastors.

If only our pastors prayed, we could see the kind of revivals we now only read about! Revival isn't dependent entirely upon our pastors. However, revival is a result of prayer, and the praying pastor is more successful in motivating his congregation to prayer than the pastor who does not pray.

Have you ever considered the possibility that the prayerlessness of the Church is a consequence of the prayerlessness of our pastors? E.M. Bounds writes, "Every preacher who does not make prayer a mighty factor in his own life and ministry is weak as a factor in God's work and is powerless to advance God's cause in the world."

Without prayer, the Word of God that is preached in our

services is not as effective as it could be. Charles Finney, the great revivalist of the last century, saw the powerful effect his prayer life had on his preaching of God's Word. In fact, while speaking of the revival that took place in Rome, New York, he once remarked, "It would be impossible for one who has never witnessed such a scene to realize what the force of the truth can be, under the power of the Holy Ghost."

The sermon is not just a series of ideas expressed in carefully selected words. It is much more than this. The sermon is an extension of the preacher's life. If prayer is not an integral part of a preacher's life, he cannot possibly set an example his people can follow. If this man does not spend much time on his knees, then he will never realize the tremendous importance of prayer. If he never sees it, he will never preach it, and there will be little or no emphasis on prayer in his church.

This is all more than hypothetical. This is an accurate analysis of the predicament of our churches today. Hopefully, pastors and church leaders who read this book will pray and begin to set their lives and churches back on course. Then maybe others who are not leaders in their churches will read this book, pray, and become leaders who will set their churches and their lives back on the right path.

In the first half of this book, we examined the causes of prayerlessness in today's church with some minor comments about how to reverse that trend. In this, the second half, we will concentrate our greatest attention to reversing this trend, not just in our personal lives, but also in our churches. We know from what was discussed in the preceding chapters that the solution to our problems is prayer. In the following chapters, we will systematically document that solution in a "how-to" format: "how to" bring revival in our church and "how to" bring revival in our own personal life.

Chapter XIII

Communicating like Christ

> *Until self-effacing men return again to spiritual leadership, we may expect a progressive deterioration in the quality of popular Christianity year after year until we reach the point where the grieved Holy Spirit withdraws like the Shekinah from the temple.*
> — Dr. A.W. Tozer, praying pastor

Do you remember the last time you delivered a sermon or a Sunday school lesson that packed all the power of a Sominex tablet? Have you ever reached the point where you just don't have anything worthwhile to teach or preach about? Thomas Paine was wrong; it's times like those that try men's souls.

Such times leave you frustrated, thinking, *Why can't I be more like Christ? He never put anyone to sleep. The fact of the matter is that when Jesus Christ spoke, everybody listened. He spoke with such authority that prostitutes and tax collectors even ended up praising God! What's more, He even got through to the stuck-up, know-it-all Pharisees. He so effectively convinced them of their sinfulness that they rejected His words and set out to stone Him on several occasions!*

If you can relate to this, I have good news for you. You can be more like Christ. In light of this, I'm going to re-phrase your question so that it asks, "Why am I not more like Christ?" In answer to the question, I feel compelled to answer, "You can't be more like Christ if you don't pray like He did." As we will soon see, prayer was the lifeblood of Jesus Christ's ministry.

Authority

One of the most potent qualities of Jesus' preaching and teaching was the authority with which He spoke.

> The people were amazed at His teaching because He taught them as one who had authority, not as the teachers of the law (Mark 1:22).

Today, many people do not understand what is meant by "authority" in this context. Although we hear much about the authority of the believer in terms of the power we may exercise over demons, we hear little about the kind of authority referred to in Mark 1:22. To even begin to understand this concept, one must first acknowledge that authority of this kind is granted because of one's position, not because of his vocal power. Since we are in Christ (that is our position), we have authority. One man's ability to project his voice further than another man does not give him greater authority.

Christians have frequently mistaken the physical manifestation of a man's voice as authority. Pentecostals are particularly notorious for this. In prayer, for example, if we are required to pray for something a second time, we will do so, only more loudly than the first time. If we are required to pray a third time, we will shout. Apparently, we have reasoned that the increased volume of our prayers will in some way serve Satan with a spiritual eviction notice, forcing him to leave. But, of course, this is erroneous. It is our authority in Christ that forces him out, not our own voices.

I became a victim of this misconception while I was teaching a prayer seminar once. After the first evening sessions, the pastor and I went out to a local restaurant for a cup of coffee. During the course of our conversation, the pastor complimented me, saying, "This is perhaps the finest teaching on prayer my church has ever heard." However, he quickly added, "But if you don't start shouting and pacing back and forth on the platform, my people simply will not believe a word you say." Despite his warning, I continued the seminar as usual, refusing to become someone I am not to accommodate these people. As the pastor warned, those people didn't believe a word I said. In fact, anyone who is familiar with my preaching style must realize by now that I left that church with the congregation rating me somewhere between a pagan and a backslider.

That church was under the impression that authority was the result of a series of physical actions. It seems that if I had employed some cheap theatrics to meet that church's criteria for authority, they would have wholeheartedly accepted my message. However, because I did not, that congregation assumed that I had nothing valid to say.

What, then, is authority? Webster defines it as "the ability to influence or command thought." As Christians (and especially as ministers!) we are in the business of influencing thought as we are constantly endeavoring to convince people of our beliefs. Any man who is successful at convincing people of his beliefs is considered an authority.

In forming our concept of authority, we should also consider the Greek word *exousia* for which we render the English word "authority" in Mark 1:22 and elsewhere in the New Testament. Exousia implies power and knowledge. In other words, we find that the person who understands authority (because of his position) can exercise his ability to influence or command thought based on his knowledge of the power available to him.

As I stated earlier, because we are in Christ we have authority. However, we struggle with exercising this authority until we fully understand the power available to us. It is this power which is one of the two basic means through which authority is realized. The second is knowledge.

> Jesus replied, "You are in error because you do
> not know the scriptures or the power of God" (Matt.
> 22:9).

Jesus knew what was wrong with the religious leaders in Jerusalem: they knew the Scriptures, but did not know anything about the power of God. This prevented them from being sincere people of God and also kept them from being good teachers. Jesus indicated here that it is necessary for a teacher to have knowledge of the Scriptures and of the power of God. That sort of teacher will influence thought.

Authority Through Knowledge

> Stop listening to instruction, my son, and you will
> stray from the words of knowledge (Prov. 19:27).

In this verse, presumably written by King Solomon, the word "instruction" is an English translation of the Hebrew word *musar.* Musar connotes chastisement and self-denial. In our contemporary colleges and universities, musar plays a significant role. Ask any conscientious college student, and he'll tell you that self-denial is a necessary element of his academic life.

Self-denial walks hand in hand with discipline, an endangered species in our self-indulgent culture. However, those few who dare to be disciplined in any given area find that they've become very knowledgeable in that area. For example, my father, who has been an automobile mechanic all his life, became knowledgeable about cars because he invested years of his life disciplining himself to study them and work on them.

As Christians, we need to practice self-denial and discipline every bit as much as scholars and skilled workers. That self-denial and discipline needs to come in the form of prayer and the study of God's Word. These disciplines yield knowledge, just as the others do. But instead of yielding knowledge about automobiles or calculus as the others do, these yield knowledge of God. God's Word provides us with knowledge of God, while prayer will help us *know* God.

If we study God's Word we will continually run into this one command: pray! If we study God's Word and, yet, don't pray, then we have "strayed from the words of knowledge by not listening to musar (discipline/instruction)." It is apathy toward this biblical admonition to pray that has brought us preachers who can quote God's Word in Hebrew and Greek, but can't convincingly preach their way out of a paper bag. They may preach with great eloquence and fabulous style, but neither their eloquence nor their style will change lives. They are talented speakers but powerless preachers. How could they be any different? Without prayer, they are cutting themselves off from one of authority's two constituents (i.e., knowledge).

> My son, if you accept my words and store up my commands within you, turning your ear to wisdom and applying your heart to understanding, and if you call out for insight and cry aloud for understanding, and if you look for it as for silver and search for it as for hidden treasure, then you will understand the fear of the Lord and find the knowledge of God (Prov. 2:1-5).

This segment of Proverbs shows us the importance of the combination of the Word of God and prayer. These two elements practiced will result in the knowledge of God. Therefore, I must discipline myself to be in prayer and the Word of God, for then only will I know God.

Authority Through Power

> Now to him who is able to do immeasurably more than all we ask or imagine, according to his power that is at work within us (Eph. 3:20).

Paul the Apostle had a healthy understanding of God's omnipotence. He understood that God is able to do anything. At times we have problems that seem as if they are going to sweep over us and drown us. We don't know how they can ever be solved. Yet the worst of them all is mere child's play for God. There is nothing He is unable to do. Yet, if this is the case, why do we not see more miracles?

Our text from Paul's letter to the church in Ephesus explains why: because God only does things in accordance with the power at work in us. If that power is vibrantly flowing through us, we will see great signs and wonders. If, on the other hand, there is no power at work in us, we will see only what the hand of man can accomplish. Our lack of miracles is nothing less than a consequence of our own spiritual power shortage. We simply do not have the necessary power at work in us, and the only One we can get that power from is God. We can receive that power only in prayer.

In Jeremiah 33:3, "the weeping prophet," as he is known, quotes the Lord as saying, "Call to me and I will answer you and show you great and mighty things which you do not know:"

This is quite simple in theory, but very difficult in practice. God has promised us great and mighty things if only we'll call to Him. When we are communing with Him, we develop an awareness of His power. The more time we spend with Him, the more we sense His power.

It is important to realize that in prayer God's power becomes a reality in our lives, not just a theology. A correct theology about God's power tells us only that God gives us power as His son. However, we will not see and experience that power until we transfer our head knowledge about God's power into heart knowledge via prayer. After prayer, our intellectual assent blossoms into a life-changing reality which will permeate our life and ministry.

All believers have this power available to them, but only those who pray are generating that power. The apostle James spoke of this power when he stated that "the effectual fervent prayer of a righteous man avails much" (James 5:16). There is one Greek word which we render as the two English words "effectual" and "fervent." This word, *energeo*, denotes the involvement of energy. Consequently, we could interpret this passage, "The energized prayer of a righteous man avails much."

I believe prayer and its interaction with our faith can be likened to a power generator. Where an earthly generator is concerned, you increase the amount of power generated by turning the handle in a designated direction. The more you turn the handle, the more power the generator puts out. Where our "faith generator" is concerned, we increase the power of our faith by turning a handle called "prayer." Prayer is a faith- builder. The more we pray, the more our faith is built up.

This is corroborated in Hebrews 12 where the writer admonishes his readers to run their spiritual race "looking unto Jesus, the author and finisher of our faith:" Looking to Jesus, as we do in prayer, builds our faith.

Thus, through the discipline of prayer we gain knowledge, and through the practice of prayer we gain power. The combination of knowledge and power enables us to communicate with great authority. We then have a much greater opportunity to command or influence thought.

The reason this is important is found back in our opening verse: "The people were amazed at his teaching because he taught them as one who had authority" (Matt. 1-22). The word "amazed" can also be interpreted "interested." As communicators, we want to interest our hearers. If we are to communicate like Christ, we must also pray like Christ.

Building Compassion

When he saw the crowds, he had compassion on them because they were harassed and helpless, like sheep without a shepherd (Matt. 9:36).

Throughout His life and earthly ministry, Jesus was a man of deep, limitless love. The compassion He continually exhibited toward others was a by-product of that love. When He taught the crowds in those arid lands, He empathized with them, grieving with them in their pain. To Him, those people were not just automatons, nameless, faceless people. No, instead, He saw them as real people with real hurts. He observed them as tragic examples of man without God.

Today, however, many teachers and preachers have little compassion for their crowds and multitudes. They look at them as just an audience. Their primary concern is putting on a performance. But this is not Jesus' way. If we are to be Christ-like in our communicating, we must be people who have compassion for those who hear us.

The apostle John wrote, "Whoever does not love does not know God because God is love" (1 John 4:8). This presents us with a problem. It seems that we cannot even pray for love. I often hear people praying for love, but I believe they are praying in error. The Bible does not command us to pray for love. That is because love is very unique. Unlike healing or finances, God will not simply bestow love upon a person just because he asks for it. God will never just plunk down love upon a person in bulk quantities. It simply doesn't work that way. If a person does not love, his lack of love is just a symptom of a much more serious problem documented in the aforementioned verse: he does not know God.

Today's saints do not need more love. What we really need is more of God. When we have love, it is because we have God. When we do not have love, it is just a side effect of our own distance from God. That is why the Lord will not answer a petition for love. If He were to just inject a person with love somehow, He would not be dealing with that person's real problem (i.e., estrangement from his Creator). This lack of love can be dealt with only after a person realizes that he needs more of God, that he needs to truly know his God.

The best and only way I know of to get to know God is to dare to spend time with Him. As we do this, we begin to sense His presence, and, subsequently, His character. As we pray consistently, that character rubs off on us until we are completely covered and filled up with it, and chief among the attributes of that character is love. From personal experience, I can state that once I'm filled with the Lord and His character, I don't have any trouble loving even my worst enemy. However, if I stay out of God's presence long enough, I struggle with loving anybody who provokes me even slightly.

Compassion has been and will always be crucial to the ministry because compassion creates a "steadfast spirit" within the teacher or preacher or a "right" spirit, as the King James Version says. King David testified to this truth in Psalm 51:10 where he pled, "Create in me a pure heart, O God, and renew a steadfast [right] spirit within me."

When a person has a right spirit, he ministers in conviction rather than condemnation. As Dick Eastman once said, "Condemnation kills, conviction cures." Conviction draws people to God, condemnation drives them away.

Romans 8:1 states that condemnation is not for the believer: "Therefore, there is now no condemnation for those who are in Christ Jesus." That doesn't promise us that we'll never have feelings of condemnation, but it does assure us that those feelings will not come from God. When God deals with us and our sin, He will use conviction, not condemnation. In this way, we will be drawn to Him and not driven away from Him.

Teachers and preachers who pray will always exude compassion, as well as a right spirit. When they speak, their message will reach down deep into the spirits of their listeners. Their words will encourage their hearers to draw nearer to God because then God will send His holy conviction down. When God's conviction results, our words have tremendous potential to influence and change lives, but that will never happen aside from prayer. Without prayer, lives and hearts will never really be changed.

I have heard "men of God" say some powerful things, but with a wrong spirit. The only substantial result was condemnation. This is so because the power of the preacher is not in his diction or in his vocabulary, but in his spirit. That is why men of prayer preach with a right, steadfast spirit and usher in conviction. The power of these men is their spirit, which is, in turn, a result of prayer.

Unfortunately, many people today are impressed with words when their main concern should be a man's spirit — who that man really is inside. As I stated earlier, we minister to others through who we are in Christ. If a man fails to develop God's character, he has nothing to offer others.

What we know *about* Jesus is really of very little importance if we do not *know* Him. If we know Jesus, we minister to others through His spirit in us. It is a spirit of love and compassion, not hate and revilement. Without that spirit, a preacher may say the correct things, but if he has a wrong spirit, only condemnation and strife will result, and the message will not be received. That is why I have always maintained that if a man is preaching in a condemning way, if you sense a heavy weight of condemnation descending on you, then he is preaching on a subject he has studied, but does not really know in his spirit.

Do not be deceived; the gifts of the spirit never prove a ministry. They work through us and can work in the life of any person to whom they are given. The fruit of the spirit, on the other hand, prove who we are. A good tree does not bear bad fruit, nor does a bad tree bear good fruit. Keep in mind that gifts are received, but fruit is developed.

Jesus was a man of deep compassion. He ministered in compassion, and He healed because of His compassion. If we are ever to minister as Jesus did, we must spend time in His presence.

Building Wisdom

In correspondence with the believers in Corinth, the apostle Paul mentioned that Jesus had become wisdom for us (1 Cor. 1:30). Therefore, any examination of Jesus' preaching must include some commentary on His wisdom, yet another factor we must consider if we truly wish to communicate as effectively as Jesus did.

Wisdom is lauded as "supreme" in Proverbs 4:7. "Therefore, get wisdom" the verse concludes. The King James Version translates the verse a bit differently by calling wisdom "the principal thing." Nowhere in the Scripture is anything else referred to as "the principal thing" In fact, throughout the Bible, those who have walked closely with the Lord have hailed wisdom as one of the most godly and most desirable of all attributes.

This "principal thing" is procured only through prayer, as James 1:15 explains: "If any of you lacks wisdom, he should ask God, who gives generously to all without finding fault, and it will be given to him." Prayer is often a pursuit of wisdom. We pray many times because we need direction, insight, and knowledge. In prayer, we receive wisdom because it draws us closer to God, the One to whom there are no mysteries, the author of all knowledge and wisdom.

An Exercise in Foolishness

It has been observed, and rightly so, that the fool says in his heart, "There is no God" (Ps. 14:1). The fool, then, has an excellent reason for not praying. The way he sees things, there's nobody to pray to, no one to hear and answer his prayers. It would be foolishness compounded for one to pray to a God he does not believe in.

If this is true, then logic dictates that the wise man, on the other hand, says in his heart, "There is a God." The wise man must pray. He knows in his heart that in prayer he can draw near to the God whose resources are endless and whose creative capacity to intervene on behalf of man is limitless.

Who is the more foolish, then? Is it the fool who insists there is no God and does not pray, or is it the "wise" man who knows that God does indeed exist and does not pray? For you to proclaim that there is a God while lacking a prayer life is to make yourself out to be a bigger fool than the most adamant atheist or the most vocal agnostic. How foolish we prove ourselves to be by not praying to the God we claim loves us and created us!

The Beginning of Wisdom

In Proverbs 2:2-3, 5 we read:

> So that you make your ear attend to wisdom and
> your heart reach out for discernment; yes, if you be-
> seech understanding, and lift your voice for discern-
> ment . . . then you will understand the fear of the Lord.

Why does fearing the Lord become important to us? Because the fear of the Lord is the beginning of wisdom. For many
years, I have made the preceding portion of Scripture a part of
my prayer life. I have asked God to give me the knowledge of
Him and to help me understand the fear of the Lord.

The fear of the Lord is by no means a new idea, but it is,
unfortunately, a rather abstract concept as far as many are concerned. I know that many believers today wonder just what this
fear of the Lord is. Does it mean cowering in a corner somewhere for fear that God is going to bang us on the head with
some kind of spiritual sledgehammer? Does it mean walking
around in a state of paranoia for fear that the Lord has a contract
out on our lives? To both questions, the answer is a definite, absolute "No!"

To fear God means to maintain an attitude of respect and
reverence toward Him. He is our Creator; we must revere Him.
He is our Father; we must honor Him. This inevitably leads us to
obedience to His commands. It would be the height of disrespect
to ignore His wishes. In accordance with our respect and honor
for Him, we obey Him. This obedience further perpetuates prayer
because we then obey God's command to pray.

So it is that prayer becomes the active practice of fearing
God. Without prayer, we cannot say that we fear God. Through
prayer, the results of fearing God develop in our lives. For example, we begin to hate evil, pride, and arrogance (Prov. 8:13). It
prolongs our lives (Prov. 10:27). It allows one to sleep satisfied,
untouched by evil (Prov. 19:23). Furthermore, we are rewarded

with riches, honor, and life (Prov. 22:4).

God teaches us the "fear of Him" as we sit patiently in His presence. Psalm 25:14 says, "The Lord confides [reveals secrets] in those who fear him; he makes his covenant known to them." This is why the fear of the Lord is the beginning of wisdom — because prayer (the fear of the Lord) gets us God, and God is wisdom. The secret of the Lord is for those who pray.

Wisdom enters the heart through prayer. While we are in prayer, God speaks to our hearts. The heart of the wise is the heart of the person of prayer. It becomes imperative for Christians to have a wise heart because wisdom helps us become better communicators.

The Book of Proverbs continues to shed light on our search for wisdom in 16:23, which declares, "A wise man's heart guides his mouth, and his lips promote instruction." The word instruction here means "persuasion." The verse could be paraphrased, "When the heart teaches a man's mouth to speak, his words become very persuasive."

This is the crux of the matter. We must be people of prayer so that wisdom will enter our hearts. Then the heart will teach the mouth to speak. When we speak from the heart, we are far more convincing than at any other time, and we are in the business of persuading people concerning the gospel. If we want to reach our maximum persuasiveness, we need to be spending as much time as possible in prayer.

The Foundation; Faithfulness

There is an important foundation upon which all this must be built. That foundation is faithfulness, the important factor that figures in to make us effective in the work of God. Compare that to unfaithfulness. In Proverbs 22:12 it says, "The eyes of the Lord watch over knowledge, but he frustrates the words of the unfaithful." When the Bible makes such a general reference to faithfulness, it is referring to the pursuit of God (which we have already found is expressed through prayer). The end result of faithfulness in the spiritual realm is intimacy with God. The faithful man, we must conclude, is, among other things, a man of prayer. Without prayer, there is no consistency in our pursuit of God.

The Scripture indicates that the unfaithful man finds his words are confused. Wisdom enters the heart through prayer. Without prayer, the heart does not teach the mouth to speak, therefore, our words become confused. There is an old proverb which tells us, "A message prepared in the intellect will only reach the intellect, but a message prepared in the heart will reach the heart."

If all we are trying to do is match wits with our audience, then we will never convince our listeners. I believe that Paul the Apostle understood this. He was a highly educated man, one who was considered an intellectual in his day. Yet he did not awe his listeners with his impressive education or extensive vocabulary. Instead, he spoke from his heart. It was the heart of man that Paul wished to change, not the intellect.

Today, we are not in need of great analytical expositions of God's Word as much as we are in need of men who seek God. Too much preaching today is dull and unconvincing because it is being preached by men who spend no time with God.

King Solomon once remarked, "Many a man claims to have unfailing love, but a faithful man who can find?" (Prov. 20:6). Human nature hasn't changed much in all these centuries. Men are still fond of forever discussing their own virtues and their own sincerity. Yet where are the men who are really faithful? Where are the people whose prime goal is to draw closer to God, which cannot be done without prayer? We need men and women who dare to pray without ceasing! At that point we can revisit the power of the gospel and come to people with signs and wonders instead of just education and polish.

Chapter XIV

The Praying
Church

The church that is not praying is playing.
— Leonard Ravenhill, revivalist

When my brother and I were teenagers, we were the original "Odd Couple." He was tall and muscular, and I was neither. He was very popular with girls. The only girls I was popular with were the girls who wanted to go out with my brother and saw me as a convenient way to reach their objective.

I always played Jerry Lewis to his Dean Martin. My brother was, of course, aware of the situation, but he never mentioned it. Finally, I brought up the subject one day, asking him how I could generate a little more popularity with the fairer sex. He suggested that I lift weights as he had. I tried it, but after several days nothing had changed so I gave up.

In those early teen years, I didn't understand the importance of consistency. If I had continued working out in the gym for an extended period, I would have seen results (physically, at least). However, in the interim, I have come to appreciate the fact that consistency is the strength of any given endeavor, particularly prayer. Consistency in prayer is a real faith-builder.

Yet when most of us get into a tight spot where we really need God, we realize then how inconsistent we really are in our Christian walk. Our faith is hindered, and we reach a point of despair. What hinders our faith? Our own disobedience. The reverse is also true. Our obedience to God (particularly In prayer) builds our faith, subsequently, we then expect God to respond to our cries for help.

I was at home doing some yard work one day when I received a phone call from a local hospital requesting that I come as quickly as possible to pray for a lady from our church who had just suffered a heart attack while at the hospital visiting her injured son. Fortunately, she received immediate treatment because she was at the hospital. While she was being treated, she kept asking the doctors to call Ron Auch to come to the hospital to pray for her.

Needless to say, I was a bit nervous on my way to the hospital. She made a point of insisting that the hospital call me at once. What was I going to really be able to do? What if I prayed and nothing happened? Heart attacks are very serious business. As I began to pray about what I was going to do, a peace which passed all understanding swept over me and I sensed the Lord saying, "Ron, you've been faithful to me in prayer. We've been alone together this very day. Allow your own faithfulness in prayer to become your strength."

With those words of comfort, I entered her room, laid my hands on her, and asked God to heal her. I didn't go through any mental gymnastics, trying to conjure up faith or force it out of my being somewhere. I didn't try to shout her body into health or forcefully push the illness from her body with my hand. I simply relaxed and believed God. Within half an hour her condition had changed so radically that the doctors decided she hadn't suffered a heart attack after all. All indications showed her to be in fine health so they had no reason to keep her in the hospital and released her shortly after that.

If I hadn't been faithful to the Lord in prayer, I probably

never would have believed that God would work such a wonder in answer to one of my prayers. I probably would have perspired profusely and wished that I had prayed more often. But that was not the case. My consistency in prayer had built my faith.

This principle works on the corporate level as well as on the individual level. If a church is consistent in prayer, that body will find that its faith in God has increased greatly. The kind of character qualities which prayer builds into an individual, it also builds into the character of the praying church. That is why it is so crucial to have some kind of daily prayer meeting in the church.

It is imperative today that we develop churches that pray, not just because of the answers that come through prayer, but for the sake of character development. In Galatians 6:9 we read, "Let us not become weary in doing good, for at the proper time we will reap a harvest if we do not give up." In prayer, we learn to "plow through" so that we can reap that harvest. The individuals who pray learn more and more about tenacity. As time goes on, they will never give up.

Minister of Prayer

I have had many different opportunities to function as a Minister of Prayer in several churches. Typically I agree to come to a church for one week a month to help them develop their prayer ministry. I will do this for one year. The following are some of the things our ministry as incorporated in many different churches:

Morning Manna

Morning Manna (MM) is a daily prayer meeting which begins at 6:00 a.m. every Monday through Friday, concluding at 8:00 a.m. Those particular hours catch people on their way to work. It's an opportunity which attracts a large number of men (due to the early hour) to this prayer meeting, which has become a powerful asset.

The first half hour is unstructured. From 6:00 until 6:30, people can come and spend time with God alone. Then from 6:30

to 7:30, an hour of structured prayer is offered, led by a member of the pastoral staff. The concluding half hour is unstructured, as was the first.

We discovered that the most effective way to help people to pray at those early hours is to offer them a structural framework in which to work. When I first started Morning Manna (MM) the full two hours were unstructured. The sanctuary was opened at 6:00 a.m., and people had the opportunity to come in and pray. We had a small group of stalwarts (5 to 15) who came and prayed each day, but it scarcely grew for three years. We then decided to provide a more structured approach. The response was decidedly favorable. Attendance increased to an average of 50 people each day.

I received a little insight into our MM prayer meeting after visiting the Full Gospel Central Church in Seoul, Korea. I noticed that Pastor Cho's church drew 20,000 people to the morning prayer meeting. Twenty-thousand people is no small crowd, and the impact of that meeting was very powerful. However, Cho's church was running 400,000 at that time. That's 5 percent of his total attendance. This seems to be a common percentage in many churches across our country. Five people out of 100 are involved in the prayer ministry of their church. If God is doing the wonderful things He is with 5 percent of His people, just think of the untapped potential that sits in our churches.

Reaching 5 Percent Attendance

It's not that any church would want to settle for just 5 percent of her people praying. It's just that many of our churches don't even have that average. One thing seems to stand out above all other things in getting the church to pray: The senior pastor made it mandatory for his pastoral staff to attend Morning Manna. He began to promote MM from the pulpit, sharing with our people that we were structuring it and that the entire pastoral staff would be there. Soon people began to respond. An old adage tells us, "As the pulpit goes, so goes the pew." I am convinced of this statement's truth. Further, I am certain that the involvement of our churches in prayer depends on our pastors' enthusiasm towards it and involvement in it.

Before the entire staff began joining in MM, I was periodically asked by laypeople attending, "Do the other pastors pray?" The average layperson assumes that his pastor is a person of prayer, but when he sees his pastor passing up opportunities to pray, he is confused. Pastors need to attend MM, if for no other reason than to reassure and encourage their congregation. If they don't they may conform to a plaque I once read which said, "There they go, so I must hasten to catch up with them and overtake them, for I am their leader."

Morning Manna Format

A four-step approach to group prayer:
1. Songs of praise and worship — 10 minutes
2. Scripture reading and confession — 10 minutes
     (read the Proverb of the day)
3. Intercession — 30 minutes
4. Praying in the harvest — 10 minutes

Details of Format

The following account details the MM format.

1. *Songs and Worship.* At 6:30, we begin the hour of structured prayer by calling everyone together into one area where we sing and worship together. This helps those who are not quite awake to wake up. It's important to be active, lest your MM group doze off like the Apostles did in the garden. That's why we encourage audible worship, singing choruses that promote worship. We usually do this for approximately 10 minutes.

2. *Scripture reading and confession.* This second step offers each individual a time of introspection and, subsequently, confession. Soul-searching and confession are extremely important on a daily basis. Without them, ministries go bad and so do people because they are no longer asking God to check their motives. The MM lender explains that they are going to have a time of private confession and introspection, to let it speak to them.

When I lead MM groups, I read what I call "the Proverb of the day." If it is the tenth day of the month, I read the tenth chapter of the Book of Proverbs. This not only brings the Word of God into the prayer time, but it also keeps one from dealing with the same sin over and over. Sometimes it is easy to pray about the same sin over and over, causing the time to get stale and boring. When we take in God's Word, the Holy Spirit has a way of pointing out things we never give thought to. I encourage every MM group to allow the Word of God to be the finger of conviction and then admonish them to spend the next several minutes praying by themselves about how the Word spoke to them. Generally, we allocate about 10 minutes for this step.

3. *Intercession.* This is the largest single portion of time during the hour. This is a time set aside for praying for others. This is really the heart of the matter. This is where one has an opportunity to share prayer requests. Because of the importance of this step, I will deal with it in great detail later in this chapter. On the average, we invest about 30 minutes in intercession.

4. *Praying in the Harvest.* This is one of the most unique and also most powerful periods of prayer we have. At this time, we ask God to give us a harvest of souls from every direction of the community, spending time facing each of the four general directions and praying for them one at a time. Importantly, we do not pray to the north, south, east, and west. Rather, we pray to God concerning each of these areas of our community.

Rev. Larry Lea first introduced this creative means of prayer. It is based upon Isaiah 43:4-6 which states:

> "Since you are precious in my sight, since you are honored and I love you, I will give other men in your place and other peoples in exchange for your life. Do not fear, for I am with you; I will bring your offspring from the east, and gather you from the west. I will say to the north, 'Give them up!' and to the south, 'Do not hold them back.' Bring my sons from afar and my daughters from the ends of the earth."

As I have already indicated, we stand and face each direction as we pray for it. When a direction has been sufficiently prayed for, the leader instructs the group to change directions. This is done until all four directions have been prayed for. The reason we do this is that it gives us the opportunity to address the specific issues unique to each part of the community.

Morning Manna Intercession Schedule

Monday: City, state, nation — 1 Timothy 2:2
Tuesday: Families — Malachi 4:6
Wednesday: World missions — Psalm 2:8
Thursday: Lost souls, revival — Psalm 85:6
Friday: Sunday's services, various church ministries
— Ephesians 5:18-21

More About Intercession

On each of the five days of the week, we have a different focus for intercession. We found it necessary to come up with a schedule to follow. Without it, there is too much repetition from one day to another. If there is no schedule, then the only other thing there is to do is to ask for prayer requests. There is certainly nothing wrong with asking for prayer requests, but if that's all we do, we usually have the same people every day with essentially the same requests. That becomes a bit dull, hollow, and meaningless after a while. We found that having a determined focus for the day keeps things from becoming dull and provides a powerful vehicle for united prayer.

Monday: City, State, Nation

[Pray] for kings and all who are in authority, in order that we aught lead a tranquil and quiet life in all godliness and dignity (1 Tim. 2-2).

Every city has problems, and every city has a governing body. As we intercede on Monday mornings, we list all our prayer requests for our city on an overhead projector as individuals make them. Along with praying about a variety of issues, we always pray for our mayor. We follow the same procedure for the state and the nation, making sure that we pray for our leaders. As soon as all the requests are listed on the overhead projector, the people are called to prayer for the next half hour, with the projector left on so that the group can refer back to it.

We have seen many exciting answers to prayer in our city. I was once returning home after conducting a prayer seminar when I noticed that one of the most notorious bars in the city had burned to the ground. The bar catered to many young people who would later try to drive the country roads in an alcoholic stupor. We were all delighted to hear that the place was put out of commission — until two weeks later when a sign was erected on the bar property announcing the intended erection of a "bigger, better" bar, paid for with their compensation from their insurance company.

I realized that something different was going to have to happen if we were going to have an effect on the problem of alcohol in our community. I challenged our people to pray about this issue every Monday when they prayed for the city, state, and nation. Four months later, the following headline blazed across the top of the front page of the local newspaper: "Times are tough for tavern keepers." The accompanying article went on to say "Times are tough for local tavern keepers. And for many of them the future isn't much brighter. That's the story nationally. That's the picture locally." A local bar owner was interviewed saying, "I wouldn't buy a tavern these days." The president of the Wisconsin Tavern League stated, "As many as 20 percent of the bars operating today will be out of business within five years." The subtitle of the article stated, "Sobering Trend Hurts Bars." Within weeks from the time we started to pray, a "sobering trend" swept through our city.

We also prayed for our city's (Kenosha) economy. The city is based on blue collar industry, having an extremely high rate of unemployment, far beyond the national average. A year after we started praying for the economy, Wisconsin Power & Light decided to construct an industrial park in Kenosha County which, within the next decade, is expected to generate 20,000 jobs.

Meanwhile, Chicago developers who own vacant land on the outskirts of Kenosha began saying that within the next ten years, they expected Kenosha to become the "hot spot" in our nation as far as employment is concerned. Can I allow our prayer group to take all the credit for this? I'm not sure. What I am sure of, though, is that things have happened exactly the way we prayed for them to happen.

Many of these things didn't happen until months after we began praying and had continued to pray. I believe that this testifies to the importance of consistency. We didn't give up just because we didn't see results within the first days, weeks, or even months. But after we persevered, we began seeing tremendous results, perhaps greater than we had ever dared hope for.

Tuesday: Families

And he shall turn the heart of the fathers to the children, and the heart of the children to their fathers (Mal. 4:6).

Broken homes are on the rise in our nation as never before. And recently, I have become aware of the situation as never before. One day while I was in a city where I was doing a prayer seminar, I noticed a car with a U-Haul trailer parked in front of a house. In front of the car was a young man in his twenties hugging what appeared to be a four-year-old boy. Both of them were sobbing, tears streaming down their cheeks. As the man attempted to stand, the little boy clung to him, trying to prevent him from leaving. It looked as if the father was saying farewell to his son for the last time. That scene is taking place thousands of times daily. It is a sad commentary on our nation. And it's breaking the hearts of children and parents alike across our nation.

The singular purpose of Tuesday's intercession is to turn the hearts of the fathers (i.e., parents) to the children. We pray for families in two ways:

(1) Each person prays for his own immediate family first. Nothing touches the heart more than the home. It is also more easy to begin praying for our own family, than for the family of someone else.

(2) Then, the floor is open to prayer requests for other families. I insist that only the initials be given for those couples who need prayer. This reduces the potential for gossip. After all, there is no need to give names and details. The Holy Spirit knows the situation intimately and can pray through us. The initials are written on the overhead projector and left up while our people go to prayer. After some time, everyone is asked to go on a prayer walk. Everyone walks through the pews and prays for families who they know sit in the same general area each week.

Wednesday: World Missions

> Ask of me, and I will make the nations your inheritance, the ends of the earth your possession (Ps. 2:8).

This is the day on which we intercede for our missionaries, also praying about other related world issues. Too many churches take no time to pray for their missionaries. This approach works against this tendency. In this way, missionaries are prayed for each week, keeping their names fresh in the minds of the congregation.

For the most part, America is guilty of giving its money but not its prayers to the missionary cause. We seem to depend on money more than anything else. In the New Testament, however, money and prayer were inseparable offerings in the Church. In Acts 10:31, an angel told Cornelius, "God has heard your prayer and remembered your gifts to the poor." Notice that the combination of his alms and his prayers were remembered by God.

In many of the churches where Morning Manna is being held, we will take the missionary plaques or cards and lay them on the table in the sanctuary. Then the people are instructed to go to the table and take one of the cards back to the place of prayer. After praying for one missionary, they can go back, return their card, and take a new one. Finally, we will list some of the major missionary "hot spots" of the world and pray for them.

Thursday: Revival

Will you not revive us again that your people may rejoice in you? (Ps. 86:6).

While attending the National Prayer Leaders Conference in Chicago, I found out some very interesting statistics concerning the historical relationship between prayer and revival in America. Comparisons were made between the rising number of prayer meetings being held in America today and the number of prayer meetings that were being held in the United States just before the great outpouring of the Holy Spirit at the turn of the last century. At that time, in the late 1800s and early 1900s, hundreds of prayer meetings were being held in Washington, D.C. Today, there are over 1,000 prayer meetings being held in Washington, D.C. every week.

Also, at the turn of the century, there was a great stirring among ministers concerning their own need to pray. Today as I travel around the country, I am seeing a similar interest. Pastors from coast to coast are becoming very concerned about their own prayer lives, but not for the same reasons as before. Church growth seems to be every pastor's "hot button." If you talk about church growth, they will listen. If you tell them prayer will make their church grow, they'll pray. However, in this current move towards prayer, pastors aren't just praying to make their churches grow.

Pastors are beginning to recall the very personal relationship they once had with God through prayer. They're realizing that their prayer lives have become consumed with nothing but the problems of the church. And they're also realizing that there's more to prayer than a quick means to church growth.

When we pray for revival, it has to be because God wants

men reconciled with himself, not just because we want a bigger church. A larger church will be the natural result of revival. Therefore, the correct prayer is the one that cries out for the salvation of the lost, not the one that begs for church growth.

Friday: Sunday's Services and Various Church Ministries

> And be not drunk with wine, wherein is excess; but be filled with the Spirit speaking to yourselves in psalms and hymns and spiritual songs, singing and making melody in your heart to the Lord. Giving thanks always for all things unto God and the Father in the name of our Lord Jesus Christ; Submitting yourselves one to another in fear of God (Eph. 5:18-21).

Friday is the last day before Sunday that we meet for prayer, so we use that time to pray for upcoming services. Often, we'll all go on a prayer walk through the church, praying for every aspect of the service. For example, as I walk past the pulpit, I will pray for the man who stands behind it on Sunday morning. In the choir loft, we pray for the choir and the director. As we walk through the pews, we pray that God will fill them with hungry souls.

We also pray for our Sunday school classes, children's church, youth group, and so forth. We encourage our pray-ers to be creative and to pray for the area of the church for which they have the greatest burden.

We have found that through this, there is a great expectancy on Sunday morning. Our pray-ers come believing God is going to do great things. There is an electricity in the air each Sunday morning because the sanctuary has been saturated with prayer. Nothing draws people to Christ more effectively than the presence of God.

One of our evangelism teams visited a couple who had visited our church for the first time. It turned out that they had never attended any church before that time. When asked about what they thought of the worship service, they said that their mouths dropped open and that they stood there utterly dumbfounded as the congregation stood to worship God. They testified that there was a spirit or presence in the sanctuary that overwhelmed them. They knew that whatever it was that was in that service was what was missing in their lives. That night the evangelism team explained what that "presence" was, and they accepted Christ.

Morning Manna has been a great lesson in patience for churches that have undertaken it. The people have learned that not everyone will come to MM. Try as they might, they just can't get everyone in the church doing it. But God has always had to work with a remnant. That has never been more true than in prayer. Yet the prayers of a few can affect many.

All-Night Prayer Meeting

There is more the church can offer in addition to MM, and the all-night prayer meeting is a dynamic opportunity for any church congregation to gather for prayer. The first Friday of every month seems to work well in many churches. However, when we began, it seemed that the monthly all-night prayer meeting was going to be a perpetual experiment.

Our first such meeting was held from 10:00 p.m. until 4:00 a.m. We soon discovered that 10:00 p.m. was just too late for most of our people to head out to a prayer meeting. In subsequent days, several people asked if the next meeting could begin earlier, so we moved the prayer meeting back two hours so that we met from 8:00 p.m. through 2:00 a.m. These hours proved to be much more successful.

Still, we observed some weak spots, in spite of increasing attendance. For example, on the average, we'd begin with 150 to 175 people, but most of them would leave by midnight. (We have always instructed our people to leave any time they wished.) At best, the final two hours of the prayer meeting became a kind of endurance test, all of us just determined to hang in there simply because none of us wanted to be called quitters.

What's more, the meeting was becoming a little dull. In

chapter one of this book, we examined the powerful gatherings the early Pentecostals had. They were exciting and dramatic. Our prayer meetings were developing into a series of "spiritual want ads." We'd gather to enumerate prayer requests and then listen to someone else pray for them. Sometimes we even spent more time explaining the prayer requests than we spent praying for them. I remember that on one occasion we spent ten minutes listening to a request and no more than two minutes praying for it. Where was that Pentecostal fire that ignited the prayer meetings of old?

I sat in my office praying about this the day after one of our all-night prayer meetings. My spirit was deeply moved with a sense of longing for that "something" that set those first generation prayer meetings ablaze. I then recalled the prayer meetings in which I had participated in Seoul, Korea, at Pastor Cho's church. At his prayer meetings, he preached a message God had laid on his heart first, and those gathered prayed as the Holy Spirit moved in their hearts about what was preached. There I saw that searching soul, that crying out to God.

Again we restructured, dealing with both of our major problems. We now conclude the prayer meetings at midnight instead of 2:00 a.m. since those last two hours had become a legalistic bondage. Secondly, we modeled our meetings after Pastor Cho's. We began much like we would for any church service, with worship and preaching. However, unlike most services, we called everyone down to the altars to pray as the Holy Spirit spoke to their hearts.

It was then that we began having prayer meetings that changed lives. We are re-discovering an old, but lost, Pentecostal art called "praying through." Our people didn't have the Holy Spirit speak to their hearts only to have them nod briefly as they put on their coats and rushed home. The Holy Spirit spoke and people responded, praying and seeking God — for the next three hours.

By all means, there is nothing wrong with protracted prayer! Many issues require extended prayer. I remember teaching a prayer seminar in Milwaukee one Friday evening during which the pastor was called out to an emergency at the hospital. It seems that one of the men from his church had arrived home from work that evening to find his wife unconscious after consuming the entire contents of her bottle of sleeping pills. The pastor arrived at the hospital just in time to hear the doctor instructing the man to prepare for the death of his wife. The drugs from the pills had entered her system and it was too late to make any attempts at pumping her stomach. And her heart would not be able to continue pumping at its current rate.

The pastor got back to the church as I was concluding the evening's session. As he was preparing to dismiss the meeting he disclosed the grim facts he had heard from the doctor minutes earlier. He asked someone in the audience to lead us in prayer. We gave it a good 45 seconds. Yet I felt God speaking to my spirit, telling me that if that woman's life was to be spared, we were not yet done. With the pastor's permission, I told the congregation what I sensed in my spirit and asked them to stay and pray. It was well after midnight when, as we were still praying, God showed me the spiritual battle that was taking place for her soul and how our protracted prayers were serving to build a hedge of protection around her. Then, I sensed a peace in my spirit that told me we had prayed it through and could stop.

The next morning, as the husband entered his wife's room, his mouth dropped open and he froze as he stared at his wife — sitting on the edge of the bed wearing a broad smile. She had been completely healed, physically and psychologically.

We are a church today which is over-preached and under-prayed. Statistics state that the average Christian prays approximately one minute each day. I don't believe any Christian sets his stop watch each day and sets out to pray for 60 seconds. Rather, it seems that we get excited about prayer and then, as the excitement subsides, gradually back away more and more until one day we realize that we have not spent a good amount of time in prayer in days or even weeks. As the Lord said to Jeremiah, "My people have forgotten me for days without number" (Jer. 2:32).

We have strayed very far from our roots. If the national

average is one minute of prayer a day, things have changed greatly from the first days of our movement. We are a movement that was founded at the altar of prayer. Today, to get our people to the altar takes a miracle. Prayer used to be the highlight of each service.

Imagine, if you will, your church in the midst of a revival. At the end of each Sunday night service, the pastor calls you to prayer around the altar. At the altar everyone prays for at least 30 minutes. Today we would think any church that prays for a half hour is having a revival. Years ago, when the church prayed, we would have said of a church that only prayed 30 minutes, "What could God possibly do in a church that prays so little?" Yet today the same 30 minutes would constitute revival in our minds because of spiritual declination.

Suppose you are one of those praying for 30 minutes every Sunday night. Even if that were the only time you prayed all week, you would surpass the national average of 1 minute a day by four times. When you multiply 30 minutes by 4 weeks, you get 2 hours a month of prayer. Multiply 2 hours a month by 12 months and you get 24 hours a year in prayer.

We have deep-seated problems and hang-ups that have literally taken years to develop. Out of 365 days we offer God one in prayer and then say, "God, why haven't You changed me?"

How about you? Are you praying today about the same spiritual problems you prayed about one year ago? If so, surely you can see how you are just spinning your wheels without ever going anywhere. There is no spiritual progress. Bear in mind that spiritual progress is directly related to the amount of time we are spending with God. Perhaps an all-night prayer meeting can be a beginning for you, a chance for you to begin praying about some of these deep-seated problems.

Service Intercessors

Charles Spurgeon has gone down in church history as one of the greatest, most effective preachers Christianity has ever seen. One of the reasons for his success was the several hundred people who were praying for him and the service, before and during it. Granted the results Spurgeon saw, service intercessors should be standard equipment in every church.

The intercessors pray strategically, mentioning each facet of the service as it begins. During the offering, they pray that God will move on the hearts of those giving, that the needs of the church will be met and that God will bless them. During the time of worship, they pray that the ministry of music will touch hearts, etc.

During the preaching, they pray for the preacher. They pray that his words will be anointed and that he will be under the direction of the Holy Spirit. As the service continues, they pray for whoever is in the service the Lord might bring to their minds.

I remember an exciting experience I had during prayer one Sunday morning as we had been interceding throughout the entire service. It was a wonderful time of fellowshipping with the Lord, especially near the end of the service as the Spirit of God seemed to descend on us in wave after wave. It was a sovereign move of God during which everyone there could testify, without hesitation, that God was there. At the same time, down in the sanctuary, 12 people were giving their hearts to the Lord.

Sermon intercessors are one of the most powerful vessels used in any service. It is their prayers that force Satan's hand back so that God may do what He wishes during the service.

Intercessors are not limited to the prayer room, either. The choir members have been instructed to find prayer partners who will pray silently in their pew as the choir is ministering. In this way, there are as many people praying as singing.

I'm sure that I'll never understand why it is so hard to get God's people to pray. People want to see God move. History shows us that every time God's people sought Him, He responded in marvelous ways. Therefore, it is logical that we should pray. Yet, by and large, we do not. For some strange reason, we search for other ways to accomplish the work of God.

But this is not a hard and fast rule. The best days are not necessarily behind us. No, indeed. For the believer who prays, the best, most exciting times with God are just ahead. We have not yet scratched the surface of God's tremendous will for us, and if we relentlessly pursue Him in prayer, we will do far more than just scratch that surface. For the praying pastor and layperson, the best is yet to come.

Other
books
by
Ron Auch . . .

Other books by Ron Auch:

Unshakable Man — A Stable Spiritual Force in the Home • The Bible says that the world needs men who will take heaven by force. That doesn't mean assaulting the Word of God and His Holiness. In fact, it means quite the opposite: This world is so vile and doomed that families are desperate for fathers and husbands who will pledge themselves to be committed warriors for truth.

Written especially for men who have a serious inner desire to be better in every area of their lives, this is not a book for those interested in casual or effortless change. Some change is hard, but the benefits are far-reaching. Auch implores men to arrive at a place of better living by paying strict attention to their responsibilities: families, marriages, and careers. $9.95

Other books by Ron Auch:

The Heart of the King • Do we know anymore what it means to yearn for God? Do our hearts ache to spend time with Him? Author Ron Auch explores the intense relationship between God and His famous servant King David, as chronicled in the 176 verses of Psalm 119. It's not enough to just pray a few minutes each week; *The Heart of the King* illustrates convincingly that "the man after God's own heart" had a heart for Him.

Auch captures the mood of King David with commentary after each verse, and challenges the reader that although world-changing leaders like David are rare, each human can have that some oneness with God.

Elegant in design, and having a substantive text, this casebound book will make an excellent gift and rich addition to anyone's collection. $12.95

Available at bookstores nationwide or contact
New Leaf Press • P.O. Box 726 • Green Forest, AR 72638

Other books by Ron Auch:

The Seven Spirits of God • The seven Spirits of God are mentioned four times in the Book of Revelation. What are they and how do they pertain to us?

The seven Spirits of God detail the biblical meaning of being "Spirit filled." God has a definite purpose in wanting His spirit to dwell within men. Peter defined it when he said, "You may participate in the (His) divine nature and escape the corruption in the world." The Spirit of God is to help us overcome the impurity of this world. This book challenges its readers to examine themselves to see if they emulate all of the fullness of God and are truly living the overcomer's life. $8.95

Available at bookstores nationwide or contact
New Leaf Press • P.O. Box 726 • Green Forest, AR 72638